Development of
Reflective Practice

A Study of Preservice Teachers

Development of Reflective Practice

A Study of Preservice Teachers

VICKI KUBLER LABOSKEY

Foreword by Nel Noddings

Teachers College, Columbia University
New York and London

Published by Teachers College Press, 1234 Amsterdam Avenue
New York, NY 10027

Library of Congress Cataloging-in-Publication Data

LaBoskey, Vicki Kubler.
    Development of reflective practice : a study of preservice
teachers / Vicki Kubler LaBoskey.
      p.   cm.
    Includes bibliographical references (p.   ) and index.
    ISBN 0-8077-3335-0. — ISBN 0-8077-3334-2 (pbk.)
     1. Student teachers—United States—Rating of—Case studies.
2. Student teachers—United States—Attitudes—Case studies.
3. Teachers—Training of—United States—Case Studies. 4. Thought
and thinking—Study and teaching (Higher)—United States—Case
studies.   I. Title.
    LB2157.U5L23—1994
    370.71'0973—dc20   93-46110
                                              CIP

ISBN 0-8077-3335-0
ISBN 0-8077-3334-2 (pbk.)

Printed on acid-free paper
Manufactured in the United States of America

98 97 96 95 94   8 7 6 5 4 3 2 1

Contents

Foreword

Educators have long been interested in reflective thinking. John Dewey saw it as an essential component of problem solving. Hullfish and Smith suggested that people fell into "types"—one of which was characterized by the tendency to engage in reflective thinking. More recently, the work of Donald Schön has made "reflection," "reflectivity," "reflective thinking," and "reflective teaching" important themes in teacher education.

In her new book, *Development of Reflective Practice*, Vicki LaBoskey looks at this long tradition both appreciatively and critically. Although she clearly believes that teacher educators should encourage their student teachers to reflect, she is not afraid to raise the question whether this can be done. Can we teach people to reflect? Under what conditions? Might there be limits to what we can do in this area? And how important is reflective thinking in teaching? Must a good teacher be reflective?

In her prize-winning study, LaBoskey identifies two sets of beginning teachers: Alert Novices (who already score high on a test of reflection) and Commonsense Thinkers (who initially score low), all registered in the same year-long teacher training program. The program is designed to produce reflective teachers. Will the Commonsense Thinkers be turned into Reflective Thinkers by the end of the program? I won't give away here the answer to this fascinating question.

LaBoskey explores the conditions under which these beginning teachers seem most likely to reflect. She identifies the topics and themes that attract their attention and sometimes throw them into agonies of reflection. She shows convincingly that reflective teachers ask "why" questions, and nonreflective teachers seldom do. The latter ask how, when, and to what standard, but they rarely ask to what end or why. Nevertheless, her Commonsense Thinkers are sometimes very good teachers; they can be skillful, well organized, and productive in the classroom.

The study produces several intriguing ideas for future research. For example, are math and science teachers generally less reflective than English and social studies teachers? If so, why? Should the answer be sought in types or in educational histories?

Finally, LaBoskey suggests that "passionate creeds" play an important role in the thinking of reflective teachers. Most of their reflection clusters around these creeds and the anomalies the teachers encounter as they try to live by and teach by their creeds.

This fascinating study should produce a wealth of new research and lively discussion among teacher educators.

Nel Noddings
Acting Dean
Lee L. Jacks Professor
Stanford University

Introduction

"The teacher education faculty in the elementary PROTEACH *program at the University of Florida have identified the development of critical reflection as the primary goal of their teacher preparation program"*
(Ross, 1987).

This claim is not unique. For the last several years teacher education programs and practices within programs have been referred to as "reflective" in orientation, aim, or outcome. More recently, many educators have become concerned about the validity of these assertions. Important questions are being asked and investigated—questions ranging from the definition of the terms *reflection* and *reflective practice* to the specific features and influences of the methods employed. Several whole volumes have been devoted to a description and analysis of reflective programs and strategies (Clift, Houston, & Pugach, 1990; Russell & Munby, 1992; Schön, 1991; Tabachnick & Zcichner, 1991; Valli, 1992).

But the call for reflection and reflective teacher education is not new. Educators at least as far back as Dewey (1904, 1910) have been suggesting that preservice teachers should be encouraged to become "thoughtful and alert students of education," rather than just proficient craftsmen. Among the arguments made for why the former is preferable is that "immediate skill may be got at the cost of power to go on growing. . . . Unless a teacher is such a student, he may continue to improve in the mechanics of school management, but he can not grow as a teacher, an inspirer and director of soul-life" (Dewey, 1904, p. 151). If nothing else, the limitations of time and opportunity within the teacher education program are arguments for the production of life-long learners.

Hullfish and Smith (1961) reiterated this message in their tellingly entitled book, *Reflective Thinking: The Method of Education*. They began with this statement: "If young people do not learn to think while in school, it is fair to ask: *How are they to keep on learning?*" (p. 3). Their claim was that "true education is concerned with the steady, unremitting, progressive development of intelligence as revealed through an increasing capacity and disposition on the part of each individual to think" (p. 132). Their argument in favor of reflective teacher education programs derives naturally from that premise: "It is but to state the obvious to note that those who intend to foster thought on the part of others must understand, first, the nature of thought and, second, how their own thought has been developed" (p. 216). In order to teach their students how to think, teachers must be able to think for themselves and understand those thought processes.

Similarly, but with even greater emphasis on moral development, Greene (1978) expressed the need for aspiring teachers to become more "wide-awake" to the moral circumstances of their lives. Only then will they be in a position to "initiate the young into critical questioning" (p. 48) or "to combat mystification" (p. 54). The implications for teacher education are clear:

> I am proposing, of course, that self-reflectiveness be encouraged, that teacher educators and their students be stimulated to think about their own thinking and to reflect upon their own reflecting. This seems to be inherently liberating and likely to invigorate their teaching and their advocacy. Also, it may well help in delineating possibilities never seen before—in the processes of futuring and choosing in which individuals must engage in order to create themselves. (p. 61)

If the arguments have been so compelling and the efforts so long-standing, why are teacher education programs still struggling with the issue of reflection? Why has reflectivity seemed such a novel idea in recent educational circles? What have been the hindrances? Erickson and MacKinnon (1991) suggest that there are many constraints on programs endeavoring to foster change in thought and practice. They group these constraints into two general categories: the situational or institutional and the personal. With regard to the former, others have also argued that both the profession of teaching and the institution of the schools operate in opposition to the goals of reflective practice. Lortie (1975), for instance, has claimed that teaching is a conservative activity, citing several potential reasons for this, including the socialization process, the reward structures, and the lack of assessment standards. He argued that such structures tend to make traditional teaching more expedient and more secure. For example, the absence of clear assessment standards causes untenured teachers to be more uneasy about evaluation and, thus, more likely to imitate previously favored people and practices.

Hullfish and Smith (1961) followed a similar line of reasoning with a focus upon the "fear of thought" as a block to progress. Their claim was that both teachers and parents find routines of habit comforting; although adults may pay lip service to the goal of helping young people learn to think, the uncertainty of the outcomes prevents them from following through. The conservative institutional and procedural structures remain unchanged. Nonetheless, Lortie, as well as Hullfish and Smith all went on to suggest that these blocks to growth might best be overcome by directing our efforts to the preservice education of reflective teachers. So the questions remain.

A second potential institutional explanation for the continuing struggle with reflection in teacher education is that we have been both unclear and inconsistent in our definition of terms. Calderhead (1989) observes that expressions currently used to refer to reflective processes in professional development "disguise a vast number of conceptual variations" (p. 43). He suggests that similar terms often derive from different theoretical foundations and thus have different implications for teacher education programs and practices. The confusion that results interferes with our ability both to design and implement successful techniques and to engage in comparative research on those efforts.

Even when we do clarify our aims and intentions with regard to reflective teacher education, we may not be doing what it is we think we are doing. In a summary of recent research on critical reflection, Sparks-Langer and Colton (1991) note that in spite of progress on the proposal of frameworks describing types of reflective thinking and the provision of techniques for developing it, "we are not completely clear on how one best promotes or assesses teacher reflection about political, ethical and moral values, beliefs, and attitudes" (p. 41). Although some reportedly reflective programs have been developed, there is still little evidence that the intended activities, interactions, and outcomes actually occur.

So it might be that our continuing uncertainty about reflective teacher education is due to structural features that discourage its development or to inadequacies in the design, implementation, or measurement of such programs. Alternatively, it might be that reflection simply cannot be taught; perhaps the constraints emanating from personal sources are as significant, or more so, than those arising from institutional sources. Perhaps an individual without an inquiry orientation cannot develop one; perhaps a novice deficient in the skills of reflection cannot acquire them. Or perhaps he or she can, but only with an effort so extraordinary and so time-consuming that the changes could not be accomplished within the confines of a teacher education program of any reasonable structure or duration.

These questions of personal constraints are especially hard to address because systematic analyses of what specific reflective strategies look like in operation with particular individuals are still uncommon in the literature. This is so despite widespread recognition of the importance of personal history, a position represented by Butt, Raymond, and Yamagishi (1988): "We consider the architecture of self that a person brings from life prior to teaching as important in its formative influences on how teaching is experienced and reconstructed" (p. 100).

The study reported in this book investigated the nature and stability of reflection in preservice teacher education and a possible means for its measurement. In order to help identify the personal factors that may contribute to or detract from the development of reflectivity, the research included an exploration of the interactions between individual beliefs, attitudes, emotions, and inquiry skills and a particular reflective strategy. To maximize the potential for the revelation of differential impact, the subjects were twelve student teachers enrolled in the same teacher education program—six of whom were rated as most reflective at the time of enrollment, the "Alert Novices," and six of whom were rated as least reflective, the "Commonsense Thinkers." The study used a measurement tool in the rating of these students, described in detail in Chapter 2, which was the result of a careful definition of reflection in preservice teacher education. The research compared and contrasted the groups and the individuals within groups on their reflective performance in the production of a series of "case investigations." The case investigation, described in Chapter 2 and at length in LaBoskey (1992), is one of many possible strategies designed to foster and reveal reflective thinking as defined in this book. A case investigation is an assignment for the student teachers similar to a case study. The details of focus and procedure vary, but the basic structure includes the identification of a problem or issue, a systematic exploration of that concern using various data-gathering and data-analysis strategies, and an interpretation of or conclusion about the evidence. The student teacher reports all stages in a case investigation write-up.

As will be fully described in Chapter 2, I rated each case investigation as reflective, unreflective, or indeterminate using detailed sets of scoring criteria similar to those employed in the original measurement tool. I also broke each case down into episodes associated with an aspect of reflective thinking incorporated in the assignment design—problem setting, means–ends analysis, or generalization; each episode also received a score. These scores served as indicators of general reflective performance by groups and individuals within those groups. In addition, I wrote case studies of each participant in an effort to discover similarities and differences in the particulars of individual thinking and the reasons for them. The data I drew on to construct these case studies included the case and episode scores, the whole-case write-ups, pre-study and post-study questionnaires, "freewrite" reactions to each case, supervisor evaluations, and interviews with some of the supervisors and participants.

This book serves several purposes. The first is to present an explicit definition of reflection in preservice teacher education and offer a means for measuring its expression in written and verbal presentation. The second is to examine the influence of initial beliefs, attitudes, emotions, and inquiry skills on attempts to engage novices in structured reflection. The final and more all-encompassing purpose is to reveal factors that may contribute to or detract from the development of reflectivity. It seems that reflection, the buzzword of the late 1980s, may already be in danger of going the way of just another educational fad—an "I tried it, but it didn't work" phenomenon. However, if we agree with Dewey, Hullfish and Smith, Greene, and many others that "pedagogy is a self-reflective activity that always must be willing to question critically what it does and what it stands for" (Van Manen, 1991, p. 10), we must prevent that passing. This book makes a contribution to that effort by providing a conceptual framework for thinking about reflective teaching and teacher education. It also provides suggestions for how we might better include and accomplish reflective goals in teacher education—goals that are passionate as well as intellectual, moral as well as practical.

I begin, in Chapter 1, with a review of what the literature tells us about the meaning of reflection in teaching and the efforts of teacher education programs with regard to reflective goals and strategies. This examination of other notions and efforts concludes with my particular definition of reflection and a conceptual framework for reflective teacher education.

Because we are in need of better means for identifying and measuring reflective processes, Chapter 2 presents the study's design and procedures. The discussion includes a detailed description and explanation of the tools I used to determine initial reflective orientations and to score reflective performance on the case investigations so that others might test, modify, or replace these instruments.

Chapter 3 reports on the results of the coding of cases and case episodes. Since the structural features of the three different case investigation assignments varied slightly, this section looks at the findings with regard to variation in case conditions. In my analysis I also consider issues of sequence.

Chapters 4 and 5 present key results from the individual case studies, the former being devoted to the Commonsense Thinkers and the latter to the Alert Novices. The case studies analyzed the case investigations and additional data with a focus upon patterns of reflective processes and attitudes for the comparison groups and the individuals within those groups both within and across case assignments.

In Chapter 4 I separate the Commonsense Thinker group into two subcategories: those with inquiry skill difficulties and those with emotional interferences. The Alert Novices did not break down into categories. Rather, Chapter 5 reveals two potential identifiers of all the Alert Novices: (1) the "passionate creeds" for teaching they bring with them and (2) their propensity for asking "why?" The chapter concludes with a focused comparison and contrast between the Commonsense Thinkers and the Alert Novices in general and in particular.

In the sixth and final chapter I discuss the potential implications of this research for policies, practice, and research regarding reflective teacher education. The discussion includes what might be gained from paying more attention to the individual student teacher and his or her particular beliefs, inquiry skills, emotional attitudes, and moral values, and from giving greater emphasis to the role of passion in teaching.

1

The What and Why of Reflection in Teacher Education

The dictionary has many definitions for the term *reflection*. Among them are these: "the production of an image by or as if by mirror; something produced by reflection; a thought, idea, or opinion formed or a remark made as a result of mediation; consideration of some subject matter, idea or purpose" (*Webster's Ninth New Collegiate Dictionary*, 1984, p. 989). These definitions sometimes refer to process and sometimes to product, and they denote varying degrees of exactness in representation. Presumably, different definitions would be invoked for different purposes. The use of such a multifaceted term in education in general and teacher education in particular poses some problems. In this chapter I explore the critical issues surrounding the notion of reflection in teacher education, consider reasons in favor of the idea despite the difficulties, and use those answers to formulate a conceptual framework for reflective teacher education.

THE QUESTIONS

One problem in the use of the term *reflection* in teacher education is that we have often not made clear which particular meaning we have had in mind. This makes intelligent discussion and comparative investigation of reflective programs, practices, or outcomes a virtual impossibility.

A second problem is that the definitions, whether implicit or explicit, are not used consistently by the theoreticians, researchers, or teacher educators who employ them. The definitional differences can be subtle and immaterial or extreme and consequential. A comparison of the conceptualizations of Cruickshank (1987; Cruickshank, Kennedy, Williams, Holton, & Fay, 1981) and Zeichner (1981–82; Zeichner & Liston, 1987; Zeichner & Tabachnick, 1991) illustrates the latter condition.

Cruickshank has developed and investigated an instructional strategy he calls "reflective teaching." He sees this as one alternative for the promotion of reflection on teaching in preservice teachers. Though this general orientation to reflection derives from Dewey, the specific features of his technique reveal a very discrepant interpretation of Dewey. Cruickshank's reflective teaching is a 60–75 minute exercise wherein teachers teach prescribed, timed lessons to one another. At the conclusion of instruction, the "learners" are tested and surveyed as to their satisfaction with the lesson. Finally, the participants discuss the process in small and large groups.

In this scenario the teachers are "reflecting" on an artificial situation, using very specific and limited instructional forms. In addition, they are focusing on the process–product relationship only and are scrutinizing the means, not the ends. Van Manen (1977, 1978) has suggested that this is one level of reflectivity, the lowest level. The other two are the social–political and the moral–ethical. Cruickshank (1987) claims that all three levels are considered in the evaluation of outcome; however, the characteristics of the exercises are not so inclusive. Although proposals have been made to expand the scope of reflection in this model to include unconscious values and attitudes and to have the lessons no longer be "content-free" (Gore, 1987), the basic structure still narrows the definition to very specific behaviors in highly controlled situations that are not representative of teaching in the real world.

The work of Zeichner and his colleagues, on the other hand, has explored an assortment of approaches for facilitating reflection about classroom teaching that is focused directly upon a combination of all three of Van Manen's levels: "Technical issues are not transcended, but become linked to considerations of the nature of and justification for educational ends and goals" (Gore & Zeichner, 1991, p. 122). They advocate programs that will produce students capable of transforming the nature of schooling so as to foster a more just and humane society. In this vision the central concerns of teacher education are to be "teaching technical skills of inquiry and fostering a disposition toward critical inquiry" (Zeichner, 1983, p. 7). The following statement should serve to clarify their definition and approach:

> In contrast to the traditional-craft orientation the inquiry-oriented approach attempts to develop in student teachers habits of active, persistent and careful examination of educational and social beliefs. The pro-

gram literature defines the reflective teacher as a person who assesses the origins and consequences of his/her educational work according to three kinds of criteria (technical, practical and critical). Student teachers are encouraged to reflect and examine the most effective and efficient means, to question the underlying assumptions embedded in educational practices and to deliberate over the ethical aspects of teaching and educational institutions. (Zeichner, Liston, Mahlios, & Gomez, 1987, p. 5)

The design of their teacher education programs has included several features aimed at encouraging this inquiry orientation, strategies that are more wide-ranging and less structured than Cruickshank's. One is a campus-based seminar where student teachers are engaged in a critical examination of educational issues and classroom practices as they arise, and another is action research. Because their definition of reflection encourages individual freedom and moral responsibility in addition to practical and technical competence, their methods include a consideration of the ends as well as the means of education in flexible, personal, and contextually embedded ways.

Cruickshank's and Zeichner's models of reflective teacher education are only two among many. A multitude of other frameworks have been developed that vary from them and from one another along a number of dimensions. Several scholars have developed ways to characterize and classify these variations (Beyer, 1991; Bullough & Gitlin, 1991; Grimmett, MacKinnon, Erickson, & Riecken, 1990; Liston & Zeichner, 1990; Tom, 1985; Valli, 1990; Zeichner & Tabachnick, 1991). The implication of such analyses is not necessarily that we ought to agree upon a single definition of reflection (though most of the above authors do note a preference for one form or a combination thereof, typically the forms at the extreme end of their continua—those forms best summarized as critical reflection). What it does indicate is that those who use the term need to specify exactly what they mean. The definition needs to be inclusive enough to allow for internal program design and evaluation and cross-study comparison.

Foundational Definitions

To create such a definition for reflection in teacher education, one does not have to begin from scratch. There are many well-constructed meanings of reflection, and though, as has already been illustrated, they tend to vary in some fairly significant ways, most have built upon the conceptions of John Dewey. According to Dewey (1910), reflection is the "active, persistent, and careful consideration of any belief or supposed form of

knowledge in the light of the grounds that support it and the further conclusions to which it tends" (p. 6). Reflection begins when an individual is
perplexed or uncertain about an idea or situation and ends with a judgment. In between the person carries out an active exploration, including
the identification of the nature of the problem, the generation of several
potential solutions, and a means–ends analysis of the alternatives. Most
critical to Dewey's theory is the notion of grounded belief:

> Reflection thus implies that something is believed in (or disbelieved in),
> not on its own direct account, but through something else which stands
> as witness, evidence, proof, voucher, warrant; that is, as *ground of be-*
> *lief.* . . . Thinking, for the purposes of this inquiry, is defined accord-
> ingly as *that operation in which present facts suggest other facts (or*
> *truths) in such a way as to induce belief in the latter upon the ground*
> *or warrant of the former.* (1910, pp. 8–9)

Such thought processes require an "attitude of suspended conclusion" (1910, p. 13). One must never accept suggestions uncritically and
must always suspend judgment during the necessary period of inquiry.
Alertness, flexibility, and curiosity are essential. In Dewey's definition, one
reflects in order to know whatever one wants to know, whenever and
wherever a state of perplexity arises. The method of reflection is a three-
step process including problem definition, means–ends analysis, and generalization that is carried out with the attitudes of open-mindedness, responsibility, and whole-heartedness.

Hullfish and Smith (1961) also present a quite thorough definition
of reflection. They build upon the notions of Dewey, but they give more
direct attention to the means by which classroom teachers can acquire
the techniques and attitudes of reflective thinking and also assist their
students in doing so. Their motives are distinctly social–political; they
believe reflective thought to be necessary to the preservation of democ-
racy. Hullfish and Smith define reflection as one form of thinking that
"differs from the looser kinds of thinking primarily by virtue of being
directed or controlled by a purpose—the solution of a problem" (p. 36).
The immediate purpose of reflection is to resolve the problem, but the
long-term purpose is the growth of the individual and the culture. Teachers are to use all means possible—for example, discovery learning,
inquiry-oriented discussion—to promote thinking in the classroom; and
if a choice must be made between coverage of content and fostering of
thought, the latter should take precedence.

Several more recent scholars have continued the effort to refine and
adapt Dewey's definition of reflection in relation to teaching and teacher

education. Kemmis (1985) posits the following definition, noteworthy for its succinct presentation of multiple dimensions:

> Reflection is a dialectical process: it looks inward at our thoughts and thought processes, and outward at the situation in which we find ourselves; when we consider the interaction of the internal and the external, our reflection orients us for further thought and action. Reflection is thus 'meta-thinking' (thinking about thinking) in which we consider the relationship between our thoughts and action in a particular context. . . . We pause to reflect because some issue arises which demands that we stop and take stock or consider before we act. We do so because the situation we are in requires consideration: how we act in it is a matter of some significance. We become aware of ourselves, in some small or large way, as agents of history. (p. 141)

In the view of Boud, Keogh, and Walker (1985), "reflection in the context of learning is a generic term for those intellectual and affective activities in which individuals engage to explore their experiences in order to lead to new understandings and appreciations" (p. 19). They stress the importance of consciousness in the process—that is, deliberate learning from experience. Although they acknowledge that reflection does occur at the unconscious level, they believe these ideas must be brought to consciousness before one can be an active decision maker. They accentuate the role of individual characteristics and aspirations in the learning process.

Goodman (1984) is notable among these scholars for his efforts to be thorough and comprehensive in his definitions and to take into account numerous relevant factors and a variety of conceptualizations. He tackles directly the relationship between reflection and teacher education by examining the three areas he considers to be relevant to the development of a theoretical association between the two: (1) the focus of reflection, (2) the process of reflective thinking, and (3) the attitudes necessary for reflective individuals. He concludes:

> What we have seen is that reflection suggests much more than taking a few minutes to think about how to keep the children quiet and on task; to the contrary, it implies a dynamic "way of being" in the classroom. First, then, reflection suggests a need to focus on substantive, rather than utilitarian, concerns. Second, a theory of reflection must legitimate and integrate both intuitive and rational thinking. Finally, certain underlying attitudes [the attitudes Dewey described as open-mindedness, responsibility, and whole-heartedness] are necessary in order to be truly reflective. If reflection is to be a worthwhile goal within teacher education, then our notion of it must be comprehensive. (p. 21)

Definitional Categories

The definition teacher educators settle upon depends in large measure on why they choose to include it in their educational programs in the first place. Some see reflection as a means (and in the extreme, *the* means) for learning both in the preservice experience and beyond (Boud et al., 1985; Dewey, 1910; Hullfish & Smith, 1961; Wildman, Niles, Magliaro, & McLaughlin, 1990). Therefore, preservice teachers must engage in reflective activities in order to learn any new ideas being presented to them and to acquire the means and motivation for sustained growth and development once the program has ended. Many with this view see reflective orientations and abilities as needing to be systematically taught, especially since structures of schooling work against their development and use and past histories tend to prevent it (Adler, 1991; Britzman, 1986; Bullough & Gitlin, 1991; Butt et al., 1988; Clandinin, 1989; Holt-Reynolds, 1992; Van Manen, 1991). Though past history tends to be an impediment to all adult learners, it is a particular challenge in the education of teachers because they have spent so many years in classrooms. The focus in this first view, reflection as a means for learning, is on reflection as a process in which preservice and inservice teachers must engage in order to learn from their experiences.

Some see, or also see, reflection as a means for engaging in professional activity, or even as the very essence of professional activity. Schön (1983, 1987, 1991) is particularly representative of this perspective, as is apparent in the title of his initial book on the topic, *The Reflective Practitioner: How Professionals Think in Action*. He describes professionals as engaged in a design process wherein they must frame and reframe problems and design and evaluate solutions using reflective thinking. Some have related good teaching to research (Baird, 1992; Barnes, 1992) and see reflection as a process of systematic inquiry. Many with this view also consider reflective thinking necessary to good teaching but less for its systems and more for its potential in discovering ever more successful ways of benefiting students (Noffke & Brennan, 1991; Noordhoff & Kleinfeld, 1990; Van Manen, 1991).

Most in this category do not see teaching as the simple transmission of knowledge; rather it is conceptualized as a complex and variable social activity in which teachers need to be able to adapt knowledge to specific situations. They hold definitions like those of Feiman-Nemser and Buchmann (1987) and Fenstermacher (1986). The former propose that "teaching, in sum, requires knowledge of subject matter, persons, and pedagogy. It demands principled and strategic thinking about ends, means, and their consequences. Most important, it requires interactive skills and serious commitment to foster student learning" (pp. 256–257). In their view the central task of teaching is the imparting of knowledge to students, but to do so, teachers must not only have content knowledge to impart, they must also know how to help groups of students learn the content and how to determine whether or not their pupils have learned it. Feiman-Nemser and Buchmann refer to the skills and orientations required for accomplishing these tasks as "pedagogical thinking and acting."

Fenstermacher (1986) asks the question: What does it mean to participate instrumentally in the education of another human being? He answers this way:

> To educate a fellow human being is to provide that person with the *means* to structure his or her own experiences in ways that keep on expanding what the person knows, has reason to doubt or believe, and understands, as well as the person's capacity for autonomous and authentic action, and the person's sense of place in history. It is not supplying the knowledge, the reasonable beliefs, and so on, but rather supplying the means to gain access to and continue the enlargement of knowledge, understanding, and so forth. (p. 46)

In contrast to Feiman-Nemser and Buchmann, Fenstermacher sees the central task of teaching not to be the bringing about of learning, but, instead, "the improvement of studenting." Education is the liberation of the mind; and in teaching teachers, the same end is sought. The task of teacher education, then, is to help teachers frame what he refers to as "the practical arguments undergirding their actions" (p. 46) and to assist them in repeatedly seeking and appraising the evidence relevant to the premises in these practical arguments. They are to become students of their own teaching.

In a similar vein, Grimmett (1988), agreeing with Donmoyer (1985), envisions teachers' efforts to understand situations as pursuits of meaning rather than pursuits of truth or fact. Shulman (1986a) points out that many have conceived of teaching as an art. He argues that if such a conception is accepted, the practice of teaching must be seen to require at least three different forms of knowledge: "knowledge of rules or principles, knowledge of particular cases, and knowledge of ways to apply appropriate rules to properly discerned cases" (p. 31). These images of teaching imply that novices need to be taught how to thoughtfully adapt, apply, and evaluate their knowledge of content and pedagogy to a particular learner in a certain context.

Another perspective also appropriate to this category is the image of teacher as facilitator of student thinking. Those with this view believe student teachers need to learn to be reflective because a central aspect of their role as educators is to develop thinking skills in their own students; they must know how to think reflectively in order to help others learn how (Anzul & Ely, 1988; Hullfish & Smith, 1961; Parsons, 1983). All these variations within the second perspective, reflection as professional practice, see reflective thinking as a definitive aspect of the profession of teaching, and, as such, it becomes a necessary component in the content of preservice teacher education.

Some see, or also see, reflection as a means for living the moral life and ultimately changing society (Adler, 1991; Britzman, 1986; Bullough & Gitlin, 1991; Gore & Zeichner, 1991; Greene, 1978). Many with this view argue that schools have served to maintain the status quo in an unjust and inequitable society. They propose that teachers need to play a role in changing this situation, and to do so, they must engage in critical reflection on "the numerous modes of masking what is happening in our society—the numerous modes of mystifying, of keeping people still" (Greene, 1978, p. 63). In this third view, reflection as moral development, teachers-to-be need to become autonomous and moral beings through critical self-reflection not only to live the moral life themselves, but to help create a more just and humane society for their students.

The literature on the topic of reflection is considerable, and the possibilities for variation in the definition and construction of reflective teacher education programs is commensurate. Thus the first task for a teacher educator wishing to design, implement, or study such a program is to answer the two related questions: What do I mean by reflection? and Why do I wish to include it?

THE ANSWERS

I do not believe in groupwork since I prefer to work on my own and have always been a good student. It worked well for me; it should work well for them.

I can't introduce relevant literature into the language arts curriculum, because my master teacher uses the basal reader.

I know that's a great method for teaching problem solving in math, but it won't work with these kids.

In my work in teacher education over the last several years I have heard student teachers making many such comments; it is comments like these that provide my main incentive for a reflective program focus. We are a judgmental lot, we humans; not only do we jump to conclusions quickly, but we seldom revise them (Buchmann & Schwille, 1983). In teacher education we have a particular problem because of the long "apprenticeship of observation" our students have experienced prior to entrance (Lortie, 1975). People come to us with strongly held views about education that may or may not be sensibly derived or consciously tested. This tendency to make snap judgments on the basis of personal experience presents a significant barrier to growth—to the learning of new ideas. It restricts the ability of student teachers to attend to the relevant particulars of context and individual need in educational situations. It limits their vision for change in educational institutions.

For me, then, the fundamental goal of teacher education is to teach novices to temper their judgments, to replace unsubstantiated opinion with what Dewey (1910) called "grounded belief"—grounded belief that is constantly in flux and open to revision. In my view, good teaching requires thoughtful, caring decision making wherein educators are able to move beyond the tendencies of their own biographies and the apparent mandates of their current circumstances to envision and consider alternative interpretations and possibilities. Good teachers are constantly making decisions and formulating ideas about educational goals, practices, and outcomes. These decisions and formulations may be done in the heat of the moment or in quiet contemplation; they may be primarily intuitive or mainly systematic and rational; and they may be reached alone or in collaboration with others. What matters most is that they are never conclusive; after their initial formulation, these decisions and ideas are subjected to careful reconsideration in light of information from current theory and practice, from feedback from the particular context, and from speculation as to the moral and ethical consequences of their results. Good teachers have the best interests of their students always in mind—but always with the perplexing and discomforting recognition that the definition and achievement of those best interests are neither clear nor singular.

I regard the means for this constant reconsideration to be reflective thinking, the images of which must provide the conceptual framework for teacher education programs aimed at its use and development (see Figure 1.1).

Initial Orientations

How difficult the goals of reflective teacher education are to achieve depends upon the entering beliefs–knowledge, values–attitudes, skills, and emotions of each prospective teacher. The literature suggests that credential candidates enter programs with strong beliefs and values about what

FIGURE 1.1 Conceptual framework for reflective teacher education

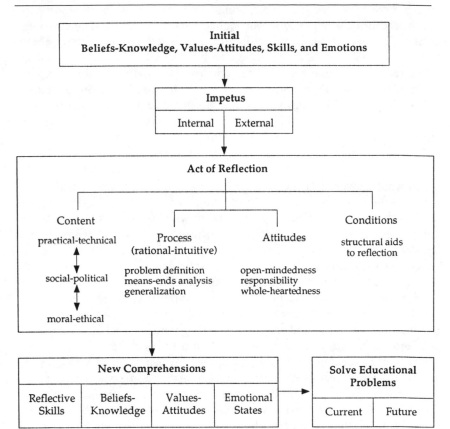

education is and ought to be, which may be a help or a hindrance (though more likely the latter) in the learning of new ideas (Adler, 1991; Britzman, 1986; Bullough & Gitlin, 1991; Butt et al., 1988; Clandinin, 1989; Feiman-Nemser & Buchmann, 1985; Holt-Reynolds, 1992; Lortie, 1975). Research also tells us that novices vary in their initial orientations toward inquiry and in their abilities for engaging in it, with the majority being less favorably inclined or prepared (Bolin, 1987; Calderhead, 1989; Gore & Zeichner, 1991; Kitchener, 1983, 1986; Lanier & Little, 1986; Russell, Munby, Spafford, & Johnston, 1988; Zeichner et al., 1987).

Other researchers and scholars remind us of the important role emotions and emotional states can play in reflective thinking and learning to teach (Clandinin, 1985; Liston & Zeichner, 1990; Noordhoff &

Kleinfeld, 1990; Richert, 1992). Theoretical and empirical work on the psychology of emotions has long argued for a connection between cognition and human emotions (Frijda, 1987; Leeper, 1969; Leventhal & Scherer, 1987; Oatley & Johnson-Laird, 1987; Shulman & Carey, 1984). Izard (1977), for instance, gives emotion a central function in the thoughts and deeds of the individual. He sees "the emotions as the chief determinants of the quality of life and as the main provider of blueprints for cognition and action" (p. 139). He suggests that the emotional process is initiated first and then the cognitive system comes very quickly into play. The two systems interact to oppose or complement each other. "In either case emotion alters perception and cognition. It is proposed that certain emotion states deautomatize or otherwise alter the structures and contents of consciousness in such a way as to preclude cognitive processes as they usually operate" (Izard, 1977, p. 157). The balance between the two systems helps to determine the effective functioning of the person, but optimal balance is not a fixed commodity—it varies with and is determined by the particular social context. Thus it is not only initial emotional states that are important; their changes must also be acknowledged and monitored.

Impetus

Because many student teachers may arrive without the internal motivation to engage in reflective thinking in general or in particular, the professional education program may have to include an external impetus in its design of reflective activities and assignments. But since the hope is that these teachers will continue to engage in reflective thinking throughout their careers, immediate participation in acts of reflection should not be the only focus. The enhancement of long-term internal inclinations ought to be a consideration as well.

Content

An act of reflection is begun either when there is a problem that the teacher cannot resolve, as Dewey (1910) suggested, or when a teacher simply wishes to rethink an educational situation or a conclusion previously reached—maybe even one with which he or she has thus far been satisfied. Though the purpose of this reconsideration may be the immediate resolution of a problem, in the ideal, the long-term goal of improving the lives of students—for creating a more just and humane society—will also be incorporated.

The content of reflection therefore needs to include all three of Van

Manen's (1977) domains: practical–technical, social–political, and moral–ethical. Like Noffke and Brennan (1991), I believe "every issue has its technical (how to), practical (what to) and critical (why) dimensions" (p. 192). Thus it is counterproductive to think of novices as passing through these domains in sequential stages of development. Nonetheless, I think the connections are not always obvious or automatic, and with the pressing demands of practical action, student teachers may need particular encouragement and assistance in considering the reasons behind and implications of their decisions and behaviors.

Process

The procedures of reflection need to include some systematic analysis of the problem, event, idea, or interpretation under reconsideration. According to Dewey (1910), individuals must proceed through three steps of reflection: (1) problem definition, (2) means–ends analysis, and (3) generalization. The process begins with a preliminary exploration of a problem. In this effort to accurately diagnose the situation, the individual must suspend judgment. Once the problem has been defined, the person entertains a variety of suggestions about how the problem might be solved. The implications of each proposal are explored through a reasoning process that selects relevant facts as evidence and applies appropriate principles to the interpretation of that data. When the results of the analysis show that one idea seems to account for the presenting conditions, whereas the others do not, a tempered judgment can be made, terminating that particular act of reflection.

One problem with this model is that it tends to overemphasize the procedures of logical thinking. The nature of the stages may need to be characterized differently. The design activities proposed by Noordhoff and Kleinfeld (1990), building on the work of Schön (1983, 1987), may prove useful in this regard. Their naming and framing of situations and issues might be substituted for problem setting; identifying goals and appraising their worth and sorting images, selecting strategies, and spinning out consequences, for means–ends analysis; and reflecting on effects and redesigning one's practice, for generalization.

But it is more than a definitional issue; I envision the whole reflective process as being far messier and more "nonalgorithmic" (Houston & Clift, 1990) than any three- or four-step formulation implies. For example, the teacher may move back and forth between issue definition and analysis of alternatives many times before reaching a tentative conclusion; anywhere during the process the teacher may have an intuitive insight that suggests a reconfiguration of all or part of his or her previous deliberations; after much consideration, no option may appear warranted, yet the teacher may still need to choose an action; or new circumstances may develop causing the teacher to temporarily abort the process.

Nonetheless, I think the stages can be useful in helping us to focus attention on potential aspects of the general process. They are not, however, all necessary to each act of reflection. Any of the "stages" may be carried out reflectively or unreflectively. Like Goodman (1991), I believe that reflective thinking is an integration of both rational and intuitive thought processes. The reflective teacher will have sensitive and creative insights but will also possess the inclination and the skills to subject those insights to careful and conscientious inspection.

Attitudes

Especially critical to my conception of the reflective process are Dewey's attitudes of open-mindedness, responsibility, and whole-heartedness. In Dewey's (1932) words, open-mindedness is an "active desire to listen to more sides than one; to give heed to the facts from whatever source they come; to give full attention to alternative possibilities; and to recognize the possibility of error even in the beliefs that are dearest to us" (p. 29). With Goodman (1991), I interpret this to mean that preservice teachers need to "examine the rationales that underlie what they [and others] may initially take for granted as right and natural in the schools" (p. 59). Without direct reference to Dewey, Van Manen (1991) presents a similar expectation: "Teachers need to be experts at alternative points-of-view, perspectives, outlooks, biases, orientations. They need to be able to see things from the child's viewpoint" (p. 193). They must keep their beliefs and values, new and old, ever open to reconsideration.

The second attitude, responsibility, means that reflective teachers must consider long-range goals as well as immediate issues. They must be willing to acknowledge that their decisions and actions have an effect on the future, but that *any* future is not acceptable. The reflective teacher must feel responsible for helping to fashion a more equitable and humane tomorrow.

The third attitude is whole-heartedness, the implications of which are well-articulated by Goodman (1991):

> This attitude gives individuals the strength to move beyond abstract notions and put their ideals into practice. Many preservice teachers express fears of making mistakes, being criticized, disturbing traditions and making changes. These fears often prevent them from acting within a given classroom or school. However, as previously mentioned, one cannot be truly reflective unless she or he is willing to take risks and

act. Wholeheartedness enables preservice teachers to work through their fears and insecurities, and thus provide a basis for action. (p. 59)

The attitudes of open-mindedness, responsibility, and whole-heartedness carry implications not only for the processes of reflection, but also for the content. A preservice teacher developing these attitudes must search out and analyze information from a variety of sources, including in that analysis the practical, the theoretical, and the moral–ethical. I believe that these notions, as interpreted above, encompass much of what is commonly referred to in the literature as critical reflection.

Conditions

These programmatic acts of reflection are carried out in a distinct context, in a certain way, and on a specific topic. Research suggests that the design and implementation of structural aids to reflection can affect the nature and quality of the outcomes of reflective endeavors. Richert (1987), for instance, found that the content of reflection varied when students reflected with and without partner–observers and with and without artifactual records of their teaching. Bolin (1987) found that reflective journals helped to shape student thinking only when the supervisory feedback was tailored to the thinking processes and content of the individual writer. The conditions under which reflection is supposed to occur make a difference; structural features matter.

The most commonly suggested strategies seem to be interpersonal interaction with a group or individual, journal writing, and practitioner research. Some have proposed that reflective thinking can be promoted in a group setting (Applegate & Shaklee, 1992; Hullfish & Smith, 1961; Kemmis, 1985; McCaleb, Borko, & Arends, 1992; Oja, Diller, Corcoran, & Andrew, 1992; Putnam & Grant, 1992; Schön, 1983; Zeichner & Liston, 1987). If designed and implemented appropriately, these group sessions are meant to enhance reflectivity by bringing more minds and multiple perspectives to bear on educational issues and by forcing individuals to bring to the surface and articulate to others their own ideas and reasoning processes.

Another frequently recommended interactive process in reflective teacher education is one-on-one conferencing with a supervisor, colleague, peer, or "coach" (Applegate & Shaklee, 1992; Candy, Harri-Augstein, & Thomas, 1985; Ciriello, Valli, & Taylor, 1992; Clift, Houston, & McCarthy, 1992; Elbaz, 1983; Main, 1985; Nolan & Huber, 1989; Richert, 1987; Russell et al., 1988; Schön, 1987; Zeichner & Liston, 1987). Most suggest that the partner needs to be supportive and skillful in detecting and fostering the skills of reflection. A composite picture of the various proposals seems to favor a safe environment, preferably over a long period of time, in which the two can frame and reframe interpretations of classroom events witnessed by both. The aims of these interactions can be for the partner to model reflective behavior for the novice; for the novice to become more aware of the various factors that might be relevant to a particular educational situation; and, ultimately, for student teachers to increase their pedagogical knowledge and/or to improve their ability to reflect on their own.

Journal writing and other forms of documentation are recommended by many, primarily as a means for keeping track of experience (Applegate & Shaklee, 1992; Bolin, 1987; Ciriello et al., 1992; Maas, 1991; McCaleb et al., 1992; Richert, 1987; Walker, 1985; Zeichner & Liston, 1987). The records or portfolios of teaching, as they are sometimes called, expand the capabilities of memory alone and allow the individual to return to the situation as often as desired or required. The process of recording events and reactions to those events is seen by many as having an additional value (see literature on "writing to learn"). Journal writers must make explicit many of their perceptions and judgments and in doing so may increase self-awareness. They may also modify some of their beliefs and interpretations as they struggle to understand and present them. The questions of focus in and external response to journal notations are variously emphasized and addressed by those who advocate this technique. Most of them agree that whatever form they take, journals help in the reenactment and reconstruction of experience, which is at the heart of reflective thinking.

One other technique often recommended in inquiry-oriented teacher education is practitioner research (Applegate & Shaklee, 1992; Barnes, 1992; Bissex, 1988; Gore, 1991; Heron, 1985; Kagan, 1992; Kemmis, 1985; Maas, 1991; McCaleb et al., 1992; Noffke & Brennan, 1991; Noffke & Zeichner, 1987; Pugach & Johnson, 1990; Ross, 1987; Teitelbaum & Britzman, 1991); preservice teachers are encouraged to engage in research in classroom settings and assisted in so doing. Perhaps the most common form of teacher research in teacher education is "action research," which has been promoted in the general teaching population with varying popularity for many years. Noffke and Zeichner (1987) describe the technique as follows: "Perhaps in its broadest sense, the term 'action research' refers to research conducted in a 'field' setting and involving those actually 'native' to the field, usually along with an 'outsider', in the solution of problems of practice" (p. 1). They qualify this description with a notation: "It is important to recognize that the plan, act, observe, reflect cycle occurs naturally in the daily work of thoughtful teachers. The difference is that in action research, teachers conduct these activities more carefully and systematically than they would normally do, ideally over a series of cycles" (p. 32). The latter is often a reason given for why teachers should be taught to do research: It is so much like what they do regularly that learning research methods can help novices become more observant, analytical teachers (Barnes, 1992; Lortie, 1975; Maas, 1991). Schön (1983) even refers to reflective professionals as "researchers in the practice context." Wehlage (1981) argues that a particular feature of research, "triangulation," is important to the development of the "self-monitoring teacher"—the teacher who is conscious of and critical about the theories that guide his or her practice. Triangulation is described as a process whereby accounts of a teaching episode are gathered from the teacher, students, and a participant observer. With access to three different perspectives, the teacher can see alternatives and implications that might not have been seen before and thereby be more "objective" about his or her teaching.

Since action research has a group discussion component, interactional method arguments, like those mentioned above, are also used by its proponents. In addition to improving the processes of reflective teaching, other advantages cited for practical research as a preservice education method are that the teacher can learn something about the topic under investigation and can develop more critical and growth-oriented attitudes in general.

The work of Wildman and Niles (1987) suggests that appropriate conditions must be provided if any reflective activities and assignments are going to be successfully completed. In particular, they stress the importance of furnishing students with adequate time for thinking. Richert's (1987) research indicates that not only does overall structure matter, but that particular details can make a difference, for example, the subject-matter background of the reflective partner. Reflective teacher education programs must be planned with careful attention to all possible features.

Outcomes

Due to the likelihood that many students will enter teacher preparation programs with beliefs–knowledge, values–attitudes, skills, and emotions that are not conducive to reflective teaching, the transformation of these interferences must be a central goal of a reflective teacher education program. The better we can define and understand what those are, the better we can change or build upon them. Reflection in teacher education is for me, then, both an end and a means. We must find ways to engage student teachers in reflective thinking in order to learn new ideas—new knowledge, beliefs, and values—from the program, and we must help candidates to develop the attitudes, skills, and emotional traits or emotional controls that will help them to become and remain reflective teachers.

CONCLUSION

My reasons for wanting to incorporate reflection in the goals and practices of teacher education programs include all three of those identified above: (1) credential students must engage in acts of reflection in order to learn during the program and beyond; (2) since the reflective process is an essential aspect of professional practice—of what teachers need to do with and for students—new teachers must develop their abilities for doing so; and (3) as moral agents, teachers-to-be need to reflect critically on the injustice and inhumanity present in our society and our educational institutions.

The theme connecting the three motives is the welfare of the children these candidates will teach, a principle embodied in Van Manen's (1991) notion of "the tact of teaching." By his definition, "tact is the practice of being oriented to others" (p. 142) or "the capacity for mindful action" (p. 122). That is, teachers demonstrate in their teaching a sensitivity to what will be most beneficial for their students. They develop their potential for tactful action through the process of thoughtful reflection, wherein they distance themselves from the situation to consider alternatives and implications.

> Thoughtful reflection discovers where unreflective action was "thoughtless," without tact. Thus the experience of reflecting on past pedagogical experience enables me to enrich, to make more thoughtful, my future pedagogical experience. This is not just an intellectual exercise, but a matter of pedagogical fitness of the whole person. What we might call "pedagogical fitness" is a cognitive and emotional and moral and sympathetic and physical preparedness. (Van Manen, 1991, pp. 205–206)

Pedagogical thoughtfulness is a central aspect of professional practice that involves learning from experience through an application of well-grounded ethical, moral, theoretical, and empirical principles. A reflective teacher education program must be concerned with the development of the beliefs–knowledge, values–attitudes, skills, and emotional tendencies that will enable future teachers to enhance the tact of their teaching through thoughtful reflection on the implications of their actions for the current and future lives of their students.

The articulation of a conceptual framework for reflective teacher education is the first step. Next is to derive and test specific practices as they interact with the beliefs–knowledge, values–attitudes, inquiry skills, and emotional states of particular student teachers. The results can lead to the improvement of structural features and to the refinement of the theoretical frame. The study reported in the following four chapters is representative of such an effort; it makes an important contribution to our understanding of what reflective teacher education programs ought to be and do in order to maximize the educational opportunities of student teachers and, ultimately, the children whom they teach.

2

How We Measure Reflection
in Teacher Education

In the growing body of literature on reflective teacher education, the work devoted to the conceptualization of the notion still far exceeds that concerned with an examination of the actual impact of programs and strategies so designed. As Ross (1990) notes, "one of the reasons for [this] lack of systematic evaluation undoubtedly is that reflection is a complex mental process that is difficult to assess" (p. 113). But to practice what we preach—to be reflective about our own work in reflective teacher education—we must try to ensure that beliefs in our structures and practices are well grounded. We need to design research programs and evaluation instruments that will allow us to determine and understand better whether or not and how we are accomplishing our goals. We need to explore more systematically the nature and stability of reflectivity in preservice teachers in order to reveal factors that may contribute to or detract from its development. Though a challenge, the effort can be facilitated by well-articulated definitions and rationales for reflective teacher education such as those presented in Chapter 1. I used my definition of *reflection,* reasons for inclusion in preservice education, and a conceptual framework for reflective teacher education to design the study reported in this book. In addition, I took some guidance from the research literature, briefly summarized below. Because of the complexity of the enterprise and the relative lack of systematic evaluation, in this chapter I share in some detail the tools and methodologies developed and employed in this research.

PREVIOUS RESEARCH

The results of the limited research that has been done on the impact of
reflective teacher education programs and structures have been mixed. In
several studies that looked at general outcome effects, the findings were
not encouraging (Korthagen, 1985; Korthagen & Verkuyl, 1987; Ross,
1987; Schön, 1987; Weade, 1987). As Calderhead (1989) put it in his
summary of the literature: "The little research relating to these areas tends
to suggest that student teachers' reflection generally remains at a fairly
superficial level even in teacher education courses which purport to be
encouraging reflective teaching" (p. 46).

In Feiman-Nemser and Buchmann's (1987) terms, beginners have a
"commonsense" view of teaching. "The central educational thesis of the
commonsense theory of knowledge is that we learn most, if not all, of
what we learn in a reliable fashion through sense experience" (Buchmann & Schwille, 1983, p. 34). Many prospective teachers have the propensity, therefore, to favor the practical over the theoretical, firsthand experience over aids to reflection. The challenge thus posed for teacher
education is not only to change novice knowledge and beliefs about
teaching but also to restructure views about how knowledge and beliefs
are acquired and evaluated in the first place.

In addition to preconceptions about teaching and learning, other attitudes, values, and propensities that novices bring with them are seen to
be significant. Borko, Livingston, McCaleb, and Mauro (1987) found
that participants who express attitudes of responsibility and control use
a problem-solving approach to planning more frequently. Schön (1987)
suggests that the student of professional practice must be "willing to suspend his disbelief" (p. 94) until he can acquire from the coach and from
experience the knowledge necessary for making informed choices. This
involves a certain degree of confidence and a tolerance for uncertainty.

Another aspect of the learner that has been discussed and investigated in relation to the growth and development of the student teacher is
cognitive or reflective ability. Some submit that novices differ in their ability to carry out the necessary mental manipulations (Calderhead, 1989;
Zeichner et al., 1987).

One scholar who has given significant and direct attention to
the explication and detection of differences in reflective ability is Karen
Kitchener (1983, 1986). Her developmental model of "reflective judgment" not only implies that different individuals may be operating at different base levels, but that performance may also vary across situations.
She has found that a person may have an "optimal level of Reflective
Judgment" but that optimal performance is influenced by environmental

factors: "Because of fatigue, lack of familiarity about the particular issue, etc., the individual may not use the highest level skill he/she can control" (1986, p. 90). She also acknowledges "that there are subtle, within-stage differences that the model doesn't capture. We know almost nothing about these differences nor whether they represent different degrees of familiarity with content, facility with logical reasoning, or personality differences" (1986, p. 86).

On a more positive note, some studies, particularly those focused upon specific program features, have found that changes do occur (Bolin, 1987; Britzman, 1989; Grossman, 1990; Nolan & Huber, 1989; Richert, 1987; Tabachnick & Zeichner, 1984; Wildman & Niles, 1987). Hollingsworth (1989) found that preservice teachers can learn ideas they do not bring with them into the program, but that appropriate contextual conditions are necessary. These conditions can be created only if teacher educators come to understand the initial beliefs of their students and use this information to guide the selection of field placements and supervisory feedback.

The cumulative results of this body of research seem to indicate a need to take a close look at the initial beliefs–knowledge, values–attitudes, skills, and emotions of student teachers. Furthermore, the questions raised by differential outcomes, particularly outcomes that imply a stability of original tendencies, suggest the importance of studying individuals who enter preservice teacher education programs with varying orientations toward inquiry. As a result, this study was designed to explore the nature and stability of reflectivity in preservice teachers by contrasting the performance of individuals who differed in their initial orientation toward and ability to reflect.

THE OVERALL DESIGN

At the time the research was undertaken, I was the Associate Director of the teacher education program at a major research university, a program that advertised itself as preparing reflective teachers. It was a fifth-year, four-quarter program at the end of which students received a single subject teaching credential and a Master's degree in Education. During the summer students participated in a campus-based Upward Bound program as observers, tutors, and team teachers in the mornings and took their university courses in the afternoons. On Friday mornings they all attended a practicum seminar. During the academic year, they student taught or interned for two high school or middle school class periods every morning in a local public or private school. Again, in the afternoons they took their university coursework. Practicum sessions continued on Wednesday evenings on a biweekly basis.

The twelve informants for the study were preservice teachers enrolled in the program concurrent with the research. The students in this teacher education program were highly motivated, verbal, and academically successful. I recognize that my research subjects may not have been representative of the larger population of beginning teachers. However, since my purpose was to generalize to theory rather than to preservice teachers in general, the atypicality of the participants was more an advantage than a problem. If we can examine the results of some of our best efforts with some of our best students, we may derive a clearer vision of what, if anything, reflective teacher education can hope to accomplish.

Two groups of preservice teachers were identified—those rated as most reflective and as least reflective on the basis of their responses to a questionnaire administered at the outset of their teacher education program. By maximizing the contrasts between the two groups, the possibility of identifying distinctive patterns of influence and performance was enhanced. Both groups carried out a series of four different assignments designed to facilitate and reveal reflective thinking. By providing opportunities for two different groups to attempt reflection under the same four conditions, a comparison of the performance of each group was made possible. In addition, the inclusion of occasions for all participants to attempt reflection under four varying conditions made possible a comparison of their performance in each circumstance.

THE INTERVENTION

Since the aim of the study was to analyze the reflective performance of preservice teachers, conditions for encouraging students to reflect and to make public that reflection needed to be provided. Thus, four (only three of which were eventually analyzed) variations of one technique—the case investigation assignment—were designed (see Appendix A for a sample assignment). A case investigation is a form of teacher research; it is less rigorous and less extensive than a case study, but it follows the same basic pattern. The case investigator is required to set a problem, gather data, analyze the data, and interpret the data for the purposes of reaching some conclusions about the problem set. All stages are then reported in a written document.

The reasons behind the selection and development of this strategy are both general and idiosyncratic. As noted in Chapter 1, practitioner research in its various forms is frequently recommended in the literature on inquiry-oriented teacher education. The primary rationale is that it is similar to what good teachers do all the time.

But I needed a particular form of teacher research, one that had the potential to both encourage and reveal reflective thinking as I had defined it. I designed the case investigation to do just that.[1] The students were introduced to the first case investigation assignment (the student case) in gradual stages over the course of the summer. Some or all of each Friday morning practicum session was devoted to instruction in the procedures for carrying out a case investigation.

First, an assistant researcher, the program supervisors, and I taught the students how to engage in the systematic observation of their case subject. We gave particular emphasis to the distinction between description and interpretation. We provided the student teachers with handouts, which included a sample format and a comprehensive explanation of the procedures. On occasion, we gave subassignments to carry out specific observations of assigned case subjects; the program supervisors led several whole- and small-group meetings in which they discussed these progressive results.[2] As time went on, the focus of these discussions became question formulation. As students shared their observations in practicum, supervisor meetings, and individual conferences, we assisted them in the identification of a particular issue of interest. We guided them in how to develop from the area of concern a specific research question that would be suitable for a brief case investigation. We made the point that the question might change over time, but that the changes should be well documented and that the final question needed to be clearly stated and thoroughly addressed.

We also gave instruction in how to carry out a research interview. In one practicum session a researcher assisting in the training and I staged a mock interview and used research questions provided by the student teachers to demonstrate interview development. We then made the assignment of doing two more observations and interviewing their Upward Bound student, provided the student consented. We also suggested that they try to interview other individuals, such as their students' teachers, dorm counselors, friends, and parents. The group discussed the pros and cons of tape recordings and note taking. At this point, we also described other sources of data: cumulative records, course pre- and posttests, and other artifacts from classwork.

Finally, we taught the student teachers how to do data analysis and case write-up. Prior to one of the practicum sessions, the guest researcher provided them with actual data from a case study she was conducting. At the meeting, they met in groups of six to discuss the data. She asked them to focus their discussion on their reactions to the material: "Consider particularly compelling passages; what do you think is going on? What is your interpretation of the material? of George? Then talk about ways in which this case study might be written up, for example, chronologically or by central themes." Afterwards we came back together as a group to share ideas and apply them to some of the developing cases of the student teachers. At this time we distributed the actual paper assignment and put samples from the previous year on reserve in the office. We did, however, encourage them to avoid the examples if at all possible and attempt to have the style and format of their particular case derive from their own question and data. The samples provided represented a wide variety of successful approaches to the assignment. Again, we provided individual and group assistance as needed during the course of data analysis and write-up. Once the case investigations were submitted, the respective supervisors[3] read them and gave thorough written feedback on the content and the form. This case investigation is referred to throughout this book as the student case.

In the fall I gave the interns their second practicum-associated case investigation assignment (the teacher case). This time the focus was to be on the teacher instead of on a student, and the teachers in question were to be themselves. They carried out this assignment during their first quarter of actual classroom teaching as an intern or student teacher[4] in a local public or private school. Though I gave little attention to further instruction in the processes of case investigation research, I did devote one practicum session to an explanation of the considerable differences between this assignment and the previous summer's case investigation. I encouraged the student teachers to identify an area of interest for them as a beginning teacher and explore it as broadly and deeply as possible in a concentrated three-week period. I posed the questions: "What is it that concerns you most about your own teaching?" or "Which of your beliefs or practices would you like to know more about or just understand better?" I also made suggestions for exploring a particularly exciting or disturbing event in the classroom. They were to draw upon information from their journals, the written observation notes of their observers, and conversations with their observers (see Appendix A for a complete description). Upon completion, the case write-ups were randomly distributed between me and the nonprogram researcher (who was also available to them for consultation during the process) for evaluation. We gave extensive written feedback on the content and form of the cases. This case investigation is referred to throughout this book as the teacher case.

The students did their third case investigation (the lesson case) during the winter quarter. This assignment was not practicum-related but was given as a requirement in one of their courses, "Foundations of

Learning for Teaching." This exercise had been a part of this course for some time; it was not developed for the purposes of this research, nor did it have any direct association with me. The students were required to work with a peer partner. Each would interview the other about the content goals of a lesson he or she planned to teach, observe the lesson being taught, and talk again with the peer teacher about observations and interpretations of the lesson. The observer then interviewed two students to try to determine how the ideas that were communicated and the instructional objectives of the lesson were represented in the minds of the learners. Following a final interview with the observed peer, the observer had to write a case analyzing what happened in the light of course readings. The respondents to these write-ups were the teaching assistants for the course. This case investigation is referred to throughout this book as the lesson case.

The interns did their fourth and final case investigation (the context case) during their fourth and final quarter in the program. I negotiated with the professors of the required sociology course to substitute a case investigation of context for their usual in-class midterm exam. The professors and I designed the assignment in a way that we thought would benefit the students, address the goals of the course, and fit with my configuration of a case investigation on context. We made the students aware of the substitution and its intent. I randomly distributed the case investigation write-ups between me and the three course teaching assistants for evaluation. I conferred with the teaching assistants on how to provide appropriate feedback to the assignment. Prior to final analysis, I eliminated this case investigation from the research design. I did so because the potential contribution to the study seemed minimized by several factors; in particular, many students appeared to be "burned out" on the process and indeed on the program itself. This case investigation is not, therefore, either used or referred to elsewhere in this book.

The written and verbal directions for all the case investigations required student teachers to follow the procedures of problem definition, means–ends analysis, and generalization in an open-minded, responsible, and whole-hearted way. Multiple perspectives and sources of evidence were to be collected and analyzed. Any conclusions reached were to be well grounded and appropriately tempered. Since all components of the process were to be included in the case write-up, many aspects of the student teachers' reflective thinking would be made available for inspection.

There is danger, of course, in relying upon the written word to reveal reflective thinking, especially if one believes reflection and action are related aspects of one process. But all of the case investigation assignments

did include practical activities; all projects involved an association between reflection and action. In addition, any conclusions drawn from the
written work of individual participants were, in subsequent case studies,
either challenged or corroborated by feedback from program supervisors
who had observed the student teachers in their classrooms. At any rate, I
agree with those who have argued for the value of sometimes looking at
thoughts apart from action. Like Van Manen (1991), I prefer to make a
distinction between reflective action and thoughtful action. In the former
the teacher distances him- or herself from the situation for the purposes
of analysis and understanding. Though its ultimate aim is to improve
practice, and therefore its eventual worth must be tested in action, reflective action still has a separateness that allows for independent study. Furthermore, I concur with Butt and colleagues (1988) that not all thought
processes—for example, the alternative behaviors considered and dis-
carded—can be revealed in action, necessitating supplementary means of
detection. I believe a verbal presentation, whether written or oral, including many of the aspects considered to be essential to the reflective process,
does hold promise for making public those aspects, as long as we recognize that it is only one lens through which to look, one piece of a larger
puzzle.

Another reason for choosing the case investigation was its potential
for adaptation; in essence this technique can, and in this study did, incorporate many other recommended strategies, such as group and dyad interaction, journal writing, and artifact accumulation. In the research design
I had three reasons for using four variations of the case investigation technique. First, Schwab (1978) has identified four commonplaces of teaching: the student, the teacher, instruction, and context. To help direct novice attention to all these important topics, each became the focus for one
of the case assignments.

Second, Fuller and Bown (1975) have observed that sequence of concern in the process of becoming a teacher needs to be considered in
teacher education. The four assignment foci were ordered to complement
the concurrent coursework and fieldwork activities of the program. In
addition, the sequence capitalized upon the developmental process: The
first case, the student case, was done prior to the start of student teaching.
Pupil concerns come last in the usual Fuller and Bown sequence, but they
are primary in pedagogical thinking. Thus this concern was purposefully
brought to their attention early and prior to their natural focus on themselves when student teaching began. When they actually started teaching,
the second case was focused on themselves as teachers; next, they carried
out a case on the instructional process in their own and a colleague's classroom; and then they did a case on the influence of context on a student.

Third, research indicates that specific program features are important. The suggestion is that variety in the content and quality of reflection can be fostered by variety of structure. I wanted to test these results by including several variations of case investigation, each with a different combination of documentation–interaction (see Table 2.1).

SUBJECT SELECTION: THE MEASUREMENT OF "SPONTANEOUS REFLECTIVITY"

To select the comparison groups for the study, I needed a means for identifying initial levels of reflectivity that would meet certain key criteria. I wanted the instrument to be as practical as possible—easily administered in a variety of contexts, for example, with large or small groups. I wanted it to assess unassisted reflectivity, or what I call "spontaneous reflection." Spontaneous reflection occurs when an individual displays reflective thinking in response to an indirect question or circumstance. For instance, if an applicant to a teacher credential program is asked why she wants to become a teacher, she is not required to employ either the processes or attitudes of reflective thinking in order to answer that question. It is not even obvious that she is being asked to display her reflective propensities, yet those processes and attitudes, if they are present, are very likely to be included in the content of her response. In contrast, situations like the case investigation have reflectivity more explicitly structured into the requirements of the task. Measurements of spontaneous reflection help to determine propensities as well as abilities, answering not only the question "Can they reflect?" but also the question "Do they tend to reflect even when not overtly asked?"

I also, of course, needed a way to measure reflectivity as I had defined it. Using my definition and conceptual framework and suggestions from the literature as to influential preconceptions and abilities, I isolated what seemed to be the most significant indicators of initial reflective, or conducive, orientations and unreflective, or nonconducive, orientations. Building on the notion proposed by Feiman-Nemser and Buchmann (1987) that entrants seem to have a commonsense view of teaching, I decided to label the more unreflective group "Commonsense Thinkers." I labeled the more reflective group "Alert Novices"; though they have a lot to learn about the teaching–learning process, they seem to possess many of the attitudes, abilities, and ideas that will facilitate rapid growth (see Table 2.2).

These indicators can, and did, serve as guides for the development of judgment criteria useful in the evaluation of a variety of assessment

TABLE 2.1 Aids to reflection for each case investigation condition

CONDITION	AIDS TO REFLECTION
Case 1 Student	• Observation notes[*] • Student-subject interviews[*] • Student products and records • Other interviews with key informants
Case 2 Teacher	• Journals[*] • Supervisor-observer interaction[*] • Supervisor consultation[*] • Peer-observer interaction[*] • Other lesson and student analysis
Case 3 Lesson	• Partner-observer interactions[*] • Teacher lesson plans • Observation notes[*] • Student interviews[*]
Case 4[†] Context	• Observation notes[*] • Interviews of student-subject[*] • Interviews of key informants[*] • Student products and records

[*] These features were required. Others were encouraged.

[†] Case 4, the context case, was not included in the final analysis.

tools. In this study I employed a questionnaire (see Appendix B) administered on the third day of the program to all 63 of the entering students (50 of whom volunteered for the study). I spent several months developing the scoring system, summarized in Table 2.3 (see Appendix C for a complete description). I gave so much attention to this process, as described in the following paragraphs, because the results determined the comparison groups on which the rest of the study was based *and* because the measurement of reflectivity is such an important and currently ill-defined task.

Since I was conducting the research on a program for which I had other responsibilities, I worked with a research assistant who assisted in

TABLE 2.2 Indicators for initial levels of reflectivity

COMMONSENSE THINKER (Unreflective)	ALERT NOVICE (Reflective)
Self-orientation (attention on self and/or subject matter)	Student orientation (attention on the needs of the children)
Short-term view	Long-term view
Reliance on personal experience in learning to teach (learn by doing; trial and error)	Differentiation of teacher and learner roles
Metaphor of teacher as transmitter	Metaphor of teacher as facilitator
Lack of awareness of need to learn; feeling of already knowing much from having been in classrooms as a student	Openness to learning; growth-oriented
	Acknowledgment of need for conclusions to be tentative; need for feedback and triangulation
Overly certain conclusions	Means-ends thinking; awareness of teaching as a moral activity
Broad generalizations	Strategic thinking
Existing structures taken as givens	Imaginative thinking
	Reasoning grounded in knowledge of self, children, and subject matter

making the students' work anonymous. She assigned a number to each respondent so that individuals were not identifiable during scoring. I tried several iterations of the scoring system and made refinements on the basis of employability, definition compatibility, and consistency. Outside raters applied and evaluated some of these iterations. Eventually, questions 2, 5, 8, 9, 10, 11, 12, and the freewrite response to a videotaped lesson from the perspective of the teacher were used in scoring. I selected these because of the richness of the responses, the appropriateness to the measurement of reflectivity, and the comparability of answers across questionnaires.

The final scoring went as follows: After several readings, I read and scored each question separately for all 50 preassessments before proceeding to the next question; then I calculated a total score for each participant, adding the scores for the eight questions; I then ranked and graphed all total scores, which resulted in a normal curve skewed to the left[5] (see Figure 2.1). Each column indicates the number of students who received a particular score. Six from each end of the curve were selected for participation in this research.[6] To check the reliability of my coding, I asked a researcher familiar with the focus of this study to code the preassessments. I first trained him in the use of the scoring instrument. Then

TABLE 2.3 Summary of pre-study questionnaire scoring criteria

SCORE	SAMPLE CRITERIA
-5	• Responses simplistic and certain • Focus upon practical issues only • Emphasis on firsthand experience as the source of learning • Teacher as transmitter of knowledge • More concern for themselves and/or the subject matter than the students; self-orientation • Short-term view
+5	• Indication of a real struggle with the issues; raises questions; evidence of uncertainty • Propensity to consider alternatives and reconsider preconceptions • Long-term view • Concern for the needs of students • Evidence of being open to learning about both practical and theoretical ideas; growth-oriented • Teacher as facilitator of learning • Recognition of the complexity of the educational enterprise • Awareness of need for tentative conclusions and multiple sources of feedback
0	Cannot be rated as +5 or -5 because they did not answer the question or because it is just too difficult to assign another score, e.g., the answer has strong features of both reflective and unreflective responses.

he coded the 12 preassessments selected for study. The inter-rater reliability for the total scores was 75%.

The 12 students selected for this research and their scores were as follows: *Commonsense Thinkers*—Andrea,[7] −35; Beth, −30; Rachel, −30; Carole, −25; Geoff, −25; and Paula, −25; *Alert Novices*—Don, +25; Gwen, +25; Heather, +25; Kim, +20; Laura, +15; and Denys, +15.[8]

THE CASE STUDIES

In order to study the nature and stability of the reflective orientations and abilities of these 12 preservice teachers, I conducted parallel case studies of the participants, which are not to be confused with the case investigations done by the student teachers. The case studies included an analysis

FIGURE 2.1 Distribution of the preassessment scores

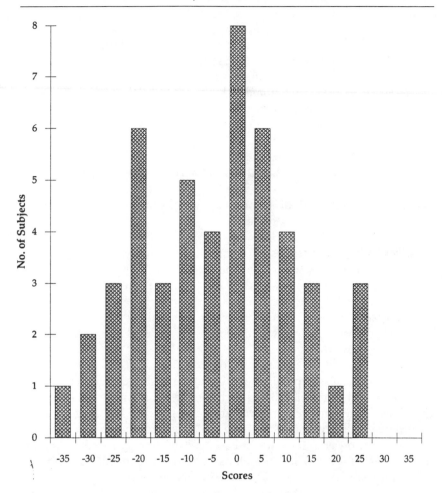

of several data sources: reflectivity scores for the case investigations; the case investigation write-ups; accompanying freewrite reactions; pre-study and post-study questionnaires; supervisor summaries; and selected interviews with supervisors and student teachers.

I chose the case study approach because the questions being explored were about an individual's pattern of performance on reflective tasks in relation to his or her initial propensities. According to Bromley (1986), "Case-studies, by definition, get as close to the subject of interest as they possibly can" (p. 23). Because reflection is a personal process and because the process of development is so little understood, a thorough and individual examination was required.

Furthermore, the study was designed to generate theory rather than to test it—theory about the nature of reflective thinking for teachers, about the role of initial reflective orientations and abilities in teacher education, and about the measurement and facilitation of reflective development. As Yin (1984) has pointed out, the case study is very appropriate to the goal of expanding and generalizing theory, especially when the interventions being explored (in this instance, the case investigations) have no clear, single set of outcomes.

Data Collection

I collected data on all 50 of the original participants prior to the determination of the 12 case study subjects.

Case investigation write-ups. The case investigation write-ups, referring to the written reports produced by the student teachers at the end of each case investigation project, were the primary data source. Both the actual content and the reflectivity scores assigned to the case investigation write-ups as wholes and to particular episodes within the write-ups were analyzed. This scoring system will be described in detail in the subsequent section, Data Analysis.

Freewrites. Each case investigation assignment also required the students to append a "thought piece" in which they reflected on personal insights gained as a consequence of the research experience. Each assignment included a brief description of the freewrite[9] requirement (see Appendix A). In the first two cases, the student case and the teacher case, I asked the authors to do the freewrite after all parts of the assignment, including the write-up, were completed. The freewrite activity was very different for the lesson case for two reasons: (1) two were required, and (2) both were to be done during the process of data gathering and prior to write-up. The first was to be written after the postobservation debriefing between the observer (the case writer) and the observed, both of whom were to freewrite on their reactions to the exercise at that point. The second was to be written after the final meeting between partners in which they discussed the results of the student interviews. Again, the task required them to note their reactions to the experience at that juncture. Because both members of the team had to do these freewrites, each subject in the study also gave two freewrites to his or her partner; these freewrites were available for data analysis if the partner was also a study volunteer.

The main purpose of these freewrites was to provide some indicators of informants' attitudes toward the reflective processes undergone in the production of the case investigations. I did not use these responses in the analysis of the case investigations themselves. I did use them in the development of the individual case studies.

Pre-study and post-study questionnaires. I used selected responses to the pre-study questionnaire administered on the third day of the program to assess the preservice teachers on their initial "spontaneous reflectivity," as described above. I analyzed all the responses for the purposes of isolating the 12 case study subjects. I administered a post-study questionnaire (see Appendix D) in February of the teacher education year, which was about two-thirds of the way through the program.[10] I used all the responses to this questionnaire in my case studies. This information helped corroborate developing theories about individual reflective processes.

Supervisor summaries. At the end of the preservice year, I asked the university supervisors to write a brief summary about each of their students describing how reflective they considered each to be at the outset and how and how much they had changed over the course of the year. I used the supervisor estimations of initial orientations to corroborate experimental group assignment resulting from the coding of the preassessments. In addition, I employed their comments in the development of the individual case studies.

Interviews. Two to three times during the year, I interviewed a subset of the 50 participants about their experiences while conducting their research. I did this in order to gain more in-depth and personal reactions to the writing of case investigations and to other program experiences. In addition, the interviews allowed the interns to clarify and expand upon the focal issues in their case write-ups. This evidence helped to verify or to refute the evaluators' interpretations of the production and content of the case investigations. These interviews were audiotaped and transcribed verbatim. Since the interviews occurred prior to preassessment coding, the final subjects in this study were not the same as the interviewees in all but three instances; Paula, Denys, and Don were case study subjects who were interviewed. There is no interview data for the other nine. Consequently, the interview data did not figure strongly in the analysis. Where relevant, these responses only served to strengthen or weaken, but not to change, conclusions drawn from other data sources.

Similarly, I interviewed half of the university supervisors prior to the preassessment coding. These interviews were also audiotaped and transcribed verbatim. The interviews took place midyear, after the supervisors had read the first two cases (the student case and the teacher case) written by each of their student participants. I asked them to react to and compare the case investigations based upon their personal knowledge of their students. I interviewed the supervisors of Heather, Denys, Carole, and Rachel, but not the others. Therefore, these interview comments also served as supplementary rather than primary data sources.

Because of these data-collection strategies, reactivity was also a concern in this study. Students reflections may have been altered by the obtrusive monitoring. However, since one of the aims of the study was to illuminate change in reflective processes, the reactivity to the intervention was more a source of data than a limitation. Whether or not students can control and modify their reflective attitudes and processes, regardless of the impetus for doing so, was a question under investigation.

Data Analysis

The first stage of data analysis involved the development and application of coding criteria for the cases. Because each case investigation was designed to include the three processes of reflective thinking—problem setting, means–ends analysis, and conclusion or generalization—I considered each case write-up to be one complete act of reflective thought. Thus I made the decision to give one score for the whole case: R for reflective, U for unreflective, or I for indeterminate. The initial coding criteria and scores derived from the original indicators (see Table 2.2), the same that were used to develop the scoring system for the preassessment questionnaires. I expanded upon these criteria and refined them during the coding of the first set of cases. Table 2.4 provides a summary of the case coding criteria. Since the case assignments were so different from one another, I developed a separate but comparable set of criteria for each case.

To check the reliability of my coding, I asked the researcher who had worked with me on the preassessments to code a subset of the case investigations. Again, I first trained him in the use of the coding instruments. In addition to the three case investigation criteria instructions, I provided him with some general guidelines for case investigation coding. He read all 12 of the student cases and assigned the same score to 10 out of the 12. He also provided written commentaries for each that allowed me to verify that we were following similar procedures in the application of the criteria. He read four additional cases from the teacher set, and we agreed on the scoring for three out of the four.

In the next stage of data analysis, I broke each case investigation into episodes. I defined an episode as a piece of the case related to problem

TABLE 2.4 Summary of case investigation coding criteria

SCORE	SAMPLE CRITERIA
Reflective	Problem setting • Shows signs of deliberation in setting the problem • Defines a problem that leaves open alternative explanations • Analyzes assumptions on which question is based • Defines a problem appropriate to a brief case investigation Means-ends analysis • Actively casts about for evidence and counterevidence • Considers a variety of alternatives • Relates evidence to the question • Carefully weighs and analyzes the implications of each piece of evidence • Applies appropriate principles to the analysis; uses more than just a "what works" criterion • Tries to suspend judgment during analysis Generalization • Follows from the evidence and from the means-ends analysis • Tempered with acknowledgment of the limitations of the study • Does not overgeneralize • Considers implications, pros and cons of results
Unreflective	Problem setting • Does not deliberate about the problem or analyze the assumptions on which it is based • Selects a problem inappropriate to a case investigation • Frames the problem in a way that implies the solution and limits exploration Means-ends analysis • Does not cultivate a variety of suggestions; leaves out some obvious possibilities • Does not use multiple data sources • Does not reconcile discrepancies; does not search for or consider counterevidence • Displays dogmatism, rigidity, prejudice, or caprice arising from routine, passion, or flippancy (fatal in Dewey's view) Generalization • Conclusions do not follow from the analysis or the evidence • Overgeneralizes • Displays too much certainty about conclusions
Indeterminate	Those cases that do not fit well into either of the above categories are to be rated as indeterminate. This usually means that parts of the case are strongly reflective and parts are strongly unreflective. No overall impression can be developed.

setting, means–ends analysis, or generalization. Each episode was fairly extensive, since it included all the sentences and paragraphs involved in the development of a particular point. The following is an example of a generalization episode from one of the student case investigations:

> Reflecting on the Upward Bound program as well as on his high school experiences, Joe was aware that his lack of self-confidence directly tied in to the teacher as well as the class atmosphere. In the Upward Bound program, Joe would regain the self-confidence he had lost during the regular school year. However, I wonder if an entire year of negative feedback can really be "erased" by only one summer of positive reinforcement. My concerns about Joe revolve around this question. If, next year, Joe has the same English teacher (which he indicated is a possibility), then I believe that his enthusiasm for English will be severely tried. Joe may decide to rely completely upon his ability to do only what is needed and nothing more. Additionally, Joe may decide that the social aspects of school are more rewarding than the academic aspects, and he may concentrate his efforts on making friends and being popular. Upward Bound and the teachers within the program may not have the same effect on Joe as they do now.

I gave each episode a score of R, U, or I, using the same basic criteria applied to the cases as a whole. The coding of episodes served two purposes. First, the more specific application of the criteria allowed for a clarification and refinement of those criteria. I modified the initial guidelines accordingly and reapplied them to the cases. They allowed for a more clear-cut decision about some of the most questionable cases, confirming the iterative nature of qualitative research. I changed the scores for five of the case investigations as a result.

Second, in the process of coding episodes I made distinctions among the three components of reflection—problem setting, means–ends analysis, and generalization. That is, I color-coded the scores for problem setting and generalization to distinguish them from the rest of the episodes. The resulting display allowed me to see where the thinking process had broken down in the unreflective cases. I was able to note the strengths and weaknesses in terms of the three reflective elements for individuals and for case assignments. After the final coding of all case investigations, I noted and summarized general trends in a conceptual memo.[11]

The results of the case investigation and episode coding are presented in Chapter 3.

The third stage of data analysis involved the production of case studies or summaries for each of the student teachers. I used the results from the first two stages of data analysis, as well as all other data sources, in the construction of these cases. The purpose was to compile all available data relevant to a depiction of each teacher's reflective abilities and orientations.

A second level of analysis for the individual summaries involved cross-case analysis. After completing the preliminary analysis of the data on the Commonsense Thinkers, I looked for patterns and themes common to all six across case investigation categories, making extensive notations of my observations. I followed the same procedure for the six Alert Novices.

A third level of analysis, also involving cross-case analysis, looked for patterns and themes within case assignment categories both within and across the comparative groups. The purpose was to attempt to identify any possible influences of the assignment structure and focus on reflective processes. This exploration also allowed me to look at the potential role of time and experience in the program, in teaching, and with the case investigation procedure.

In the process of doing this cross-case analysis I employed two techniques used by Grossman (1990) and recommended by Miles and Huberman (1984): data displays and conceptual memos. Throughout all stages of data analysis, I developed several charts to display the data. As with Grossman, these charts served two purposes. The first was to uncover missing data. When I displayed portions of the data from the case studies, for instance, I found that one set of cells for the Alert Novices were empty for the Commonsense Thinkers. Following the recursive process of qualitative data analysis, I then went back to the data in an attempt to locate the relevant information.

The second purpose of the displays was to illuminate patterns that did not emerge in preliminary analyses. Often I attempted several iterations of the same data before a definitive pattern was revealed. The episode data described above underwent this type of manipulation. Different displays of the same data sometimes proved helpful in uncovering more than one relevant pattern embedded within a single data set.

I also used conceptual memos as a common analytic tool to summarize findings, note developing themes and patterns, and posit theories to explain relationships. Some of the memos were short and informal, whereas others were longer and more systematically produced, especially those written following the completion of the cross-case analyses. I saved the interim memos and reviewed them frequently. Miles and Huberman (1984) propose that "memos are always *conceptual* in intent. They do not just report data, but they tie different pieces of data together in a cluster, or they show that a particular piece of data is an instance of a general concept" (p. 69). These memos would often lead me back to the data in search of evidence to confirm or disconfirm the proposed interpretations. Such efforts to disprove my conclusions sometimes stimulated the production of new displays and new conceptualizations.

The results of the cross-case analyses are reported in Chapters 4 and 5.

CONCLUSION

As Ross (1990) has noted, "reflection is a complex mental process that is difficult to assess" (p. 113). The tools and methods described above represent one effort to meet the challenge of more systematic evaluation. These do not, of course, constitute the final answer; they are in much need of further testing, general modification, and contextual adaptation. Nonetheless, they did reveal personal factors that seem to contribute to or detract from the development of reflectivity in preservice teachers, giving us a better understanding of the nature of reflective thinking and the ways in which it might be measured and facilitated.

3

A Look at the Case Investigations

The Alert Novices, on the whole, wrote reflective case investigations, whereas the Commonsense Thinkers did not. This finding suggests that the initial differences between the two groups remained stable, raising more doubts about the teachability of reflection. Even after substantial participation in a program aimed at facilitating reflection, and even on tasks systematically structured to produce reflection, the Commonsense Thinkers had trouble reflecting. Although this is discouraging, an exploration of the details of the reflective efforts of the Alert Novices and the Commonsense Thinkers, both as groups and as individuals, reveals trends and characteristics that are suggestive of solutions. In the next three chapters I share the results of that exploration. I begin here with an examination of the scores for the case investigations as wholes and the three types of episodes within the case investigations: problem setting, means–ends analysis, and generalization. Two factors emerge as particularly salient in the interpretation of these scores: case investigation progression and case investigation structure.

CASE INVESTIGATION PROGRESSION

Each of the case investigations was given a score of either R for reflective, U for unreflective, or I for indeterminate. A look at the progressive scores of both individuals (Table 3.1) and comparison groups (Table 3.2) reveals that changes in performance cannot be explained solely by the notion of improvement over time.[1] Although the Alert Novices, both the group as a whole and the individual participants, did get better over time, the com-

TABLE 3.1 Results of case investigation coding

		Student Case	Teacher Case	Lesson Case
Alert Novices	Laura	U	R	R
	Heather	U	I	R
	Gwen	R	R	R
	Don	R	R	R
	Kim	I	R	R
	Denys	R	R	R
Common-sense Thinkers	Rachel	R	I	U
	Andrea	U	R	R
	Paula	U	U	U
	Geoff	U	R	I
	Beth	U	U	U
	Carole	U	I	U

R=Reflective　　　　U=Unreflective　　　　I=Indeterminate

monsense interns did not. The commonsense group as a whole did slightly better on the second case investigation (the teacher case) than on either of the other two; the outcomes for the first (the student case) and last (the lesson case) cases were very similar in terms of overall score. As far as individuals go, there were five very different sequences, only one of which, Andrea's, might be associated with an "improvement over time" explanation.

An examination of the episode scores supports the conjecture that outcomes cannot be explained by time alone. As mentioned earlier, the case investigations were broken down into episodes, each of which represented one of the three components of reflection: problem setting, means–ends analysis, or generalization. In the problem-setting stage the individ-

TABLE 3.2 Summary of case investigation coding results by comparison groups

	Case Scores for Alert Novices			Case Scores for Commonsense Thinkers		
	R	U	I	R	U	I
Student Case	3	2	1	1	5	0
Teacher Case	5	0	1	2	2	2
Lesson Case	6	0	0	1	4	1
Totals	14	2	2	4	11	3

R=Reflective   U=Unreflective   I=Indeterminate

ual establishes the parameters for a particular issue, concern, or question. For instance, in her teacher case, Kim identified honesty in the classroom as a goal and set her problem as one of figuring out what she really meant by that goal and what she might do to achieve it. In a means–ends analysis, the author considers alternative solutions, explanations, and evidence for the resolution of the problem identified. Kim explored various interpretations of the term *honesty* and what the implications of each interpretation would be for classroom practice. Each option under consideration was isolated as a separate episode. Generalization includes attempts to draw conclusions about the question raised. Kim decided that honesty was a more complex issue than she had first thought and that she needed to continue to adapt her goal. Each episode was given a score of R, U, or I. The results of the episode scoring are summarized in Tables 3.3, 3.4, and 3.5 (see Appendices E and F for the itemized results).[2]

With regard to problem setting, both groups improved over time. For the Alert Novice group, problem setting in the teacher case improved over problem setting in the student case; problem-setting scores in the lesson case were very similar to those in the teacher case, except there was one unreflective score instead of one indeterminate. Only one individual in the Alert Novice group did not follow this pattern—Laura. She had a score

TABLE 3.3 Summary of problem setting episode results by case investigations

		Alert Novices	Commonsense Thinkers	Totals
Student Case	R	3	1	4
	U	3	3	6
	I	0	1	1
	Mixed	0	0	0
	None	0	1	1
Teacher Case	R	5	3	8
	U	0	2	2
	I	1	0	1
	Mixed	0	0	0
	None	0	1	1
Lesson Case	R	5	3	8
	U	1	1	2
	I	0	0	0
	Mixed	0	2 R & U	2
	None	0	0	0

R=Reflective   U=Unreflective   I=Indeterminate

TABLE 3.4 Summary of means–ends analysis episode results by case investigations

		Alert Novices	Commonsense Thinkers	Totals
Student Case	R	42	15	67
	U	22	36	58
	I	11	9	20
	Mixed	2 R & U	0	2
	None	0	0	0
Teacher Case	R	43	27	70
	U	12	21	33
	I	7	9	16
	Mixed	1 R & U, 1R & I	2 R & U	4
	None	0	0	0
Lesson Case	R	55	24	79
	U	10	39	49
	I	8	1	9
	Mixed	2 R & U	0	2
	None	0	0	0

R=Reflective   U=Unreflective   I=Indeterminate

TABLE 3.5 Summary of generalization episode results by case investigations

		Alert Novices	Commonsense Thinkers	Totals
Student Case	R	2	1	3
	U	3	3	6
	I	0	0	0
	Mixed	1 R & U	0	1
	None	0	2	2
Teacher Case	R	4	3	7
	U	1	3	4
	I	1	0	1
	Mixed	0	0	0
	None	0	0	0
Lesson Case	R	3	0	3
	U	0	2	2
	I	0	0	0
	Mixed	3 R & U	2 R & U 1 R & I	6
	None	0	1	1

R=Reflective   U=Unreflective   I=Indeterminate

of unreflective for problem setting on the student case, improved to reflective on the teacher case, but then went back to unreflective on the lesson case (Appendix E).

For the commonsense group as a whole, the problem setting for each case was slightly better than for the prior case (see Table 3.3). This could not be said of all the individuals in that group, however, where, again, the specific sequences were very mixed. Only two, Paula and Andrea, had a straightforward improvement pattern (Appendix F).

Patterns in the data for the means–ends analysis stage were not so evident; the episodes were more numerous and the scores more variable. Nonetheless, the Alert Novice means–ends analysis scores did indicate improvement over time, both as a group and as individuals, except for Don, who did the worst in the teacher case.

The commonsense group in general did better on the teacher case than they did on either of the other two. However, the individual scores were very mixed. Andrea, Paula, and Geoff did follow the group progression by doing best on the teacher case; Beth's scores showed almost no improvement at all; Rachel's scores went progressively down; only Carole's scores indicated improvement over time.

Trends for the generalization stage also were not easily defined; in several instances the participant drew more than one conclusion, and these multiple conclusions were not always given the same score, resulting in several (7 out of 36) mixed scores. Combining the Alert Novices with the Commonsense Thinkers, the results were as follows: Although the solely unreflective conclusions went progressively down from six to four to two, the solely reflective conclusions went from three up to seven and then back down to three; thus there was not a clear pattern of improvement overall (Table 3.5).

Similarly, the separate pattern for the Alert Novice group showed a steady decline in unreflective conclusions, but the reflective conclusions went from two up to four and then down to three. The Alert Novice individual sequences for this stage were more mixed than this group's sequences for the whole cases or for problem setting; four out of the six showed improvement over time (Appendix E).

The commonsense group showed only a slight decrease in unreflective conclusions over time, going from three to three to two. As with the Alert Novice and the combined scores, a roller-coaster pattern occurred with the commonsense reflective conclusions; these went from one up to three and then all the way down to zero. Only one individual, Carole, steadily improved over time, and it was a very moderate pattern; her generalization scores went from U to U to 1R/2U (Appendix F).

CASE INVESTIGATION STRUCTURE

Each of the case investigations had a slightly different structure; the data sources and the procedural requirements were not identical. These structural variations seemed to affect the case investigation and episode scores in a number of ways. Both the teacher case and the lesson case were more directed than the student case, especially in terms of the problem-setting stage. The teacher case required the use of experienced observers in defining the problem; phase two of the assignment asked the interns to meet with their university supervisors to identify developing ideas and issues. In the lesson case the problem was in essence defined for them: to analyze and explain the learning of two students as measured by student interviews. Since the problem setting scores were better in general for the teacher and the lesson case, this guidance may have helped.

The generalization stage appeared to be more problematic than the problem-setting stage, especially in the lesson case. The conclusions for this case investigation were to be drawn from an analysis of the possible association between student learning outcomes and the lesson as planned and implemented by the teacher using the course readings. The sophisticated thinking required for this process may have presented some difficulties, especially for the commonsense participants, as will be discussed in Chapter 4.

In general, both groups of preservice teachers performed least well on the student case: This case produced more unreflective case investigations and fewer reflective ones than either of the other two. In contrast, the Commonsense Thinkers in particular seemed to do best with the teacher case. What about those case investigation assignments may have caused that to happen?

The Student Case

Data from three different interviews shed some light on the differences between the student case and the teacher case. The first was from an interview with Don, a teacher from the Alert Novice group. He thought that the teacher case was more valuable than the student case because it was easier to get involved with his own concerns than with those of another: "I felt much more attached to the subject that I was writing about. I mean, it was a part of my life everyday." He noted elsewhere in the interview that because of his psychology background and his major in adolescent development, he did not get as much out of the first case investigation as other people may have; he had "worked a lot with adolescent age kids before. . . . So for me it was not any great revelation." What is really interesting to note, however, is that, in terms of episode scores, Don was one of only two in the study (Rachel was the other) who performed the best on the student case. His expertise in this area may have overridden his lack of interest.

Aaron, a supervisor, agreed in his interview with Don's comparative valuation of the two cases, but for slightly different reasons: "So my sense is they probably got more out of [the teacher case] in some ways because they had more experience to base it on. . . . I think in the summer they are so new at it and there was a real, I don't know, a reluctance or something, or sensitivity, you know, how personally involved do we get with these kids." He was suggesting first that interns may have had more trouble with the student case because they had had limited classroom experience with adolescents at the time of the assignment. He was also proposing that the preservice teachers may have been hesitant about intruding too much into the lives of their student subjects and thus may have had difficulty collecting the necessary data.

Denys, another Alert Novice, disagreed in an interview with both of the above and felt that he got more out of the student case:

> Well, as I said in there, trying to sort out, as you're looking at someone else, you can step back at least a little bit. But trying to sort out what's going on in your head is very difficult because you're so intimately involved and since you're trying to analyze cause and effect things, it's really pretty difficult. I mean, you might come up with a cause and effect connection but who knows if it's really hitting or not.

Denys produced a reflective case investigation in both categories. Even though he preferred the student case, his teacher case was in general more reflectively written (75% reflective episodes in the teacher case as opposed to 62% reflective in the student case), except for the generalization part. He confused some terms in the teacher case conclusion, and it was rated as indeterminate. The problem setting for the student case was rated as unreflective, but reflective for the teacher case. Perhaps the attitude expressed above was helpful in enhancing Denys's reflectivity on the teacher case because the doubts he admitted to are consistent with my definition of reflective thinking. One also does not know if "it's really hitting or not" in a "more objective" investigation such as the student case; for the teacher case he at least recognized this limitation.

Taken together, these comments provide several possible explanations for why the student case was more problematic. First, in dealing with the student case, the preservice teachers were experiencing the process of case investigation for the first time. Regardless of the fact that they had received fairly extensive instruction in case investigation procedures, they were new to the enterprise. This explanation leads to an expectation of improvement over time, however, and thus is not sufficient to explain the results.

A second, and related, potential explanation is that the student teachers had had insufficient classroom experience with adolescents to help them understand and interpret the circumstances from the perspective of an educator, as the assignment required. Lortie (1975) suggests that novices' understandings of the classroom derive from their experiences as students:

> It is improbable that many students learn to see teaching in an ends–means frame or that they normally take an analytic stance toward it. Students are undoubtedly impressed by some teacher actions and not by others, but one would not expect them to view the differences in a pedagogical, explanatory way. What students learn about teaching, then, is intuitive and initiative rather than explicit and analytical; it is based on individual personalities rather than pedagogical principles. (p. 62)

Student teachers thus enter teacher education programs with powerful preconceptions about life in classrooms that are based upon judgments made as pedagogically naive youngsters, inhibiting their ability to interpret the behavior of students under observation from a professional viewpoint.

Third, student teachers might enter teacher education programs with other preconceptions that could interfere with their interpretations of student data, in particular preconceptions about race and gender. As Feiman-Nemser and Buchmann (1985) found in the case of Janice, some students have negative stereotypes about males and females and about minorities that are not easily changed. Novices like Janice tend to distort new information in ways that will support their earlier beliefs. The students who participated in the study reported in this book were in the main Caucasian (10 out of the final 12), whereas all except one of the Upward Bound students whom they studied were people of color. Thus this factor may have interfered with reflectivity in the student case for some individuals such as Geoff and Carole. Geoff, who investigated the question "Does John's Mexican heritage prevent him from succeeding in school in particular and in America in general?" made several naive, broad, and unsubstantiated statements. His implicit and unanalyzed assumption was that if minority students act like "typical" American students, success in school and in life will then be easy and guaranteed. He not only did not question the validity of this goal for a student of color; he also manipulated his data to support this initial belief, as shown in the following:

> Living in what I suspect is a mostly Hispanic community, John was never made to feel out of place as he was growing up. Even if his older brothers didn't carve a niche within the community, John's background was so typical of the neighborhood that there is no reason to believe that he should have been struggling to fit into American society.

Carole attempted to understand why Marie, her case investigation subject, had no ambitions for college, whereas her older brother did. Marie was Taiwanese, and Carole hypothesized that "there was some sort of cultural sex bias that accounted for the difference." Carole admitted that finding concrete data on the issue would be nearly impossible. Although she attempted to look elsewhere for potential explanations, in the end she felt compelled to reaffirm her initial views even though her evidence was not supportive of them:

> It is hard to determine the influence the Taiwanese culture has on Marie's self-concept. I believe there is some residue of chauvinism, of female deference to the male. I wonder about her mother, a nurse living alone, away from her children; what kind of counteracting force does one "strong" female have in the mind of a girl raised in a highly patriarchal culture? And how much will living in America affect her self-image? All of these are hard to measure, even if they are assumed to be valid questions. And yes, they are questions similar to the ones I originally intended to pursue.

At least Carole's latter comments show some signs of hesitation and an awareness of her unwarranted return to the original proposition. She returned, but she did so with questions rather than an assertion.

Fourth, the model of Fuller and Bown (1975) might explain the student case results by suggesting that novices would have trouble focusing on the needs of the students at such an early stage in their preservice teacher education program because concerns about pupils usually occur last in the process of becoming a teacher. This theory was acknowledged in the design of this study; the student case was assigned first in an attempt to minimize this effect by having the preservice teachers focus on student concerns before they had actually started teaching. The hope was that the beginning teachers might move more quickly to this important stage by focusing on a student before their natural concerns for survival could interfere. The effort may not have been successful. One problem may have been that even prior to actually teaching, novices tend to have trouble observing their students from a teacher perspective. Fuller and Bown describe "preteaching" concerns this way:

> Fresh from the pupil role, education students who have never taught are concerned about pupils, that is, about themselves. They identify realistically with pupils, but with teachers only in fantasy. They have not experienced the realities of the teaching role. Education courses which deal with the teacher's realities seem to them "irrelevant." The identification with pupils manifests itself at the beginning of observation, when they are often unsympathetic, even hostile, critics of the classroom teacher whom they are observing. They have not yet, as one student observed to us, "gone over to the enemy." (p. 38)

The reflectivity of the student teachers may have been inhibited by this tendency to overidentify with their case investigation subjects. Andrea's student case freewrite is very revealing along these lines:

> I looked at this assignment in the beginning as [the university's] form of busy work for its interns. I had no desire to observe students. I came to [this university] to learn how to be a teacher, not a researcher. It was very difficult for me to focus my energy and attention on one student. As a matter of fact, it was even harder for me to pay attention to my student because he was quiet and somewhat reserved. He was not a great conversationalist, he was not quick and witty, and he slept during many of the classes. The interview I had with him was cold and stilted. Other interns ate and played with their students. I did none of these things. I didn't feel comfortable with my student. My student was just an object to be studied through as impersonable a process as possible. I reduced my student to an object similar to a paramecium I would study under my microscope. I studied him and I analyzed him. However, he never became a multidimensional person or "real" in my eyes. There was a thick icy cold wall that existed between the two of us and this summer this wall was not broken down. My student was very reserved and gave me the impression that he was not interested in opening up to me.
>
> My immediate impression to this realization was that I wish [the program] had given me a student who was outgoing, witty, athletic, and college bound or the opposite extreme—some student who was a vocal future recidivist. I had basically given it up for lost

> that I was going to learn a lot about my student. However, I then
> began to reflect upon the feelings this student was evoking in me.
> These feelings were deep inadequacies in my own personality. I
> wanted to be outgoing, I want to be witty, and I wanted to be popu-
> lar. Myself and my student were more alike than different and I dis-
> liked the parts of me I saw in him. I think this is a valuable insight
> to my psychological make-up and now that I have this awareness, I
> will be able to slowly take steps to change myself into a person I
> like better. In doing this, I will become a more effective teacher.

Indeed this revelation did prove to be important in Andrea's development, as will be discussed in Chapter 4, but for the purposes of the student case, this association with and "dislike" of her subject did prevent her from gathering much relevant data and may have contributed to an unreflective case investigation.

Heather also identified with her student, and though the identification was more positive, the association was still an interference. Heather revealed in her associated freewrite that she felt there were many similarities between her and "Mary." "I felt that we are quite similar in that we both seemed to have matured at an early age, and that the maturation was due, in part, to the development of sophisticated belief structures." The consequence of this overempathizing was frequent broad leaps in the interpretation of Mary's comments and behaviors. As her supervisor respondent noted, Heather made several "bold assertions" that were unsubstantiated and untempered. The following is one of many such examples:

> Mary has no problem with self-expression. But I was often aware
> of what might be construed as shifts in mood or tone that sneak up
> on her and almost catch her off guard, to which she responded by
> quickly recollecting herself. I often saw the young girl struggling to
> break out of the reserved persona she had created for herself, but
> she was always kept in check by the woman she wanted to be.

Heather's student case was replete with such overinterpretation, and as a result it was one of the more unreflective case investigations in the study. With 70% unreflective episodes, it was the most unreflective case investigation written by an Alert Novice.

A fifth possible explanation for why the student cases were least reflectively written is that the preservice teachers were reluctant to intrude into the lives of their student subjects, as Aaron, a social studies supervisor, mentioned in his interview. Such a hesitancy might have prevented them from gathering the necessary data.

This point is relevant to the lesson case also; the subject for that case investigation was a program peer. Several participants seemed to have trouble criticizing their partner in the case investigation write-up. Beth ignored the fact that one of the two students interviewed had not learned as expected and simply praised the lesson on the basis of the one who did learn. Geoff focused on student inattentiveness and lack of sophistication in his explanation for minimal student learning, rather than on the content of his peer's lesson. Rachel ignored student learning altogether and discussed instead the students' description and praise of the teacher's pedagogical techniques. Paula made direct mention of this difficulty in one of her lesson case freewrites: "How do I analyze this whole process without sounding overly critical about Karl's teaching?"

The Teacher Case

The commonsense group seemed to do best on the teacher case. One reason may be that the teacher case was the one case investigation where the focus was on themselves. They did not have to worry about intruding on another's life in the process of gathering data, nor did they have to worry about insulting a peer in a written document. The teacher case also fit well with Fuller and Bown's (1975) model of the developing teacher's sequence of concerns. Beginning teachers are most concerned about their own survival. In this case investigation the student teachers were allowed to acknowledge and explore those fears, perhaps granting them a certain legitimacy.

Another strength of the teacher case may have been the number and nature of the aids to reflection included in the assignment structure. The teacher case had more support systems than the others. In particular, the aids to reflection included journal writing and talking with two different partners who had observed the class. Richert (1987) has found that such social and artifactual aids influence the depth and clarity of reflection. Journal writing is one type of teaching artifact that can contribute to the establishment of an "audit trail" of classroom experiences (Bolin, 1987). Richert suggests that such documentation might help teachers to remember classroom events and to focus their thinking on the issues present in the artifact. Conversation with someone who had observed their teaching was also found to assist in the reconstruction of classroom events and served to extend the novices' focus to more general aspects of teaching and learning. She did discover, however, that the specifics of the partnership were important, in particular the degree of safety in the relationship. The details of these associations may have been influential on the outcomes for both the teacher and the lesson case.

CONCLUSION

The overall case investigation scores for the Alert Novices did improve over time. Perhaps for them the first case investigation assignment would always be the weakest because it is a necessary first step. Or perhaps other features of the student case, as discussed above, would always make the student case more difficult, no matter when it appeared in the program. Experimentation with the order of the assignments would be necessary to answer this question and is recommended for future research, especially since the implications of the two outcomes would be very different.

The structural variation in the case investigations did seem to be a desirable feature for the Alert Novices for two reasons. First, the three who produced reflective cases in all three instances did have the benefit of reflecting about three different but important "commonplaces of teaching" (Schwab, 1978)—the student, the teacher, and the lesson. Second, as illustrated in the above comments of Don and Denys (two of the Alert Novices who produced Reflective cases in all three instances), the personal enjoyment and degree of enlightenment varied for individuals. As Richert (1987) suggests:

> Different opportunities and structures for reflection suggest breadth not only in reflection content, but also an expanded repertoire of reflection styles for teachers. In designing the teacher education curriculum with a variety of reflection opportunities, teacher educators challenge novices to think in new ways and about a broader scope of educational concerns, thus enhancing the novices' preparation and capability for reflective practice. (p. 177)

For Alert Novices who enter teacher education programs with reflective propensities and abilities, these expansion exercises may be quite appropriate and productive.

The commonsense group did not exhibit a pattern of improvement over time. In fact, these individuals did not reflect well under any of the conditions; only 22% of all the case investigations they produced were rated as reflective. For the Commonsense Thinkers a case investigation designed to model reflective thinking did not in most instances foster such reflective thinking; so, to a certain degree, the assignment variation was for them a moot point.

The data suggest, however, that certain structural features do seem to provide valuable assistance to Commonsense Thinkers. Problem formulation was specified clearly in the lesson case, and five of the commonsense subjects were able to obtain a reflective score for at least a portion of the problem-setting stage. Areas needing more assistance and particular attention also emerged from the data. In only 36% of all case investigations were the authors able to draw reflective conclusions. (See Table 3.6 for a summary of results for the three components of reflection—problem setting, means–ends analysis, and generalization.)

The commonsense group produced only four reflective case investigations, but those four were spread over all three case investigations. Since every assignment worked for someone, the case investigation structure

TABLE 3.6 Summary of case investigation episode results for the three components of the reflective process

		Alert Novices	Commonsense Thinkers	Totals
Problem setting	R	16 76%	15 63%	31 69%
	U	4 19%	8 33%	12 27%
	I	1 5%	1 4%	2 4%
Means/ends Analysis	R	139 65%	64 35%	203 52%
	U	46 22%	98 54%	144 37%
	I	27 13%	19 11%	46 11%
Generalization	R	13 52%	8 36%	21 45%
	U	11 44%	13 59%	24 51%
	I	1 4%	1 5%	2 4%

R=Reflective   U=Unreflective   I=Indeterminate

alone is not as important as the interaction between the case investigation and the person. These associations and the other variations in individual patterns suggest a need to analyze each student teacher separately. The task for Chapters 4 and 5 will be to explore individual differences both within and across comparison groups.

4

The Commonsense Thinkers

Some students will learn no matter how poorly you teach and some will never learn despite your best efforts.

(Geoff)

The results of the case coding indicated that in general Alert Novices performed differently in the writing of case investigations than did Commonsense Thinkers. Alert Novices were more likely than Commonsense Thinkers to produce a reflective case, regardless of the specific structure of the assignment. They also carried out the tasks of problem setting and generalization in a reflective manner more often. These findings indicate that initial reflective abilities and orientations tend to remain stable during preservice teacher education. However, the scores do not provide us with information about the particular ways in which the thinking processes of the two groups differ. They do not tell us how the express nature of prior reflectivity interacts with the case investigation tasks. Nor do they account for the similarities and differences among individual participants. For instance, the overall scores cannot tell us why Heather, an Alert Novice, and Geoff, a Commonsense Thinker, both produced one reflective, one unreflective, and one indeterminate case.

Answering these questions requires more in-depth information about the beliefs–knowledge, values–attitudes, inquiry skills, and emotional states and traits of the student teachers and about their particular responses to the reflective tasks. This chapter presents such information about the six Commonsense Thinkers. Their case studies reveal that the individuals in this category are unreflective in different ways and for different reasons. Most significantly, the six seem to be divisible into two distinct groups: those deficient in inquiry skills and those with attitudinal or emotional interference.

INQUIRY SKILL DIFFICULTIES

Carole, Paula, and Beth all seemed to be deficient in their ability to carry out reflective thinking as it has been defined in this book, but the nature of their weaknesses varied.

Carole

Carole was adept at describing and analyzing the structural features of a situation or a problem, but she had trouble bringing to the surface the possible sources of her dilemmas. She had even greater difficulty integrating information into a conclusion about or solution for the problem identified. As her supervisor put it in his summary evaluation: "She has a good analytical mind; she can observe a situation and beautifully document the flaws. But she's weak at synthesizing." In his midyear interview, he had expressed a similar perspective. In discussing Carole's teacher case, in which she told of her frustrations with her placement school's regimented curriculum, he made the following comments:

> There was something in there [on] . . . how she's a reflective teacher to a point. She's reflecting on the constraints but she's not reflecting on what she can do about them . . . in a sense, her paper did do some reflection on the system but not enough on what she can do to be strong within that system. . . . No question that Carole is the weakest of the nine people that I'm involved with, no question, hands down. . . . [She's] been resisting a lot of things and I can't get at it exactly. . . . And a lot of it has to do with this idea that she was under a lot of constraints in Taft's system last semester. That's no longer a valid argument at all for her teaching, because she is now teaching a senior elective, two sections of junior–senior elective with no hurdles, none of the constraints that she has described and she has documented. . . . Very slow at being able to apply the theory that has been presented to her, very slow at it. And, ahh, in fact, I just remembered the theme that she was going to deal with in her case study that she really should have pursued. It was her problem in being a synthetic learner, that she's an analytic learner, she could take a particular problem and focus on it and solve it. And her writing is very strong. . . . But when she has to synthesize,

pull three pieces together or take a piece from her "Curriculum and Instruction" course and a piece from a practicum session and see how they might bring some important bearings on her class, [inaudible]. And she's talked about how the other student teachers seem so creative and so quick to creativity, this is what she should have explored because this is her main problem. I don't think she's really open to criticism fully; this resistance is defensiveness. I can't separate out what's a lack of effort—genuine effort—and what's a bailing out because she's afraid; I don't know. But there have just been a number of really, really funny things of sort of backing away sorts of things. And it seems like she backed away from that issue once again, and it's interesting how she chose to write about the system, how that system's providing her with constraints rather than reflecting herself. Well, anyway, so is she a reflective teacher? It seems she is reflecting on, she documents problems and she can document her own problems even . . . her reflections in her plan notebook are raw, "This lesson really stunk today, I couldn't get . . .", you know, this kind of thing . . . she's amazingly honest in reporting things that I would be embarrassed to report to somebody. So I don't think she has a sense of her power and what she can do to change and be stronger. And I don't think she's aware of how she can pull on tools that are available to her. . . . Carole [and two of his other supervisees] debrief in ways that disturb me, their own solo debriefings, their own sort of comments after their lessons. They rip their lessons in a way that, I can't pin down what the problem is, but it's like, "Yeah, that really stunk; I really bombed on that today." But there's not a sense of, I don't have the confidence in them yet that they can fix that situation, that they know what to do, how to think about that, to move beyond it.

Although the supervisor was basing his judgment on extensive interaction with Carole over a whole year's time, it still represents a single perspective. However, other evidence in the data helps corroborate this position. In fact, Carole's own words seem to support the notion that she has trouble moving beyond the descriptive, or "analytical," phase. In her post-study questionnaire, she responded this way to a question about whether or not the program helps students to be reflective: "Yes, we are reflective and the program encourages us, but the reflection tends to be surface level (there's a lot of forced reflection—not bad, but not directed)—I'd prefer to delve down into layers of my teaching—need help burrowing." She acknowledged a need for help in digging beneath the surface of her problems, more (or at least different) help than the program had been providing her.

In her freewrite reaction to the teacher case, Carole noted that she was "astonished" by the results of her tally of the number of periods her class was required to spend on preparing for and taking district examinations. "Although I had known the number of days was high, I had no idea that they would constitute over half the semester." She commended herself, and rightly so, for a meticulous documentation of a regimented curriculum. However, she concluded with this statement: "Having been able to stand back and regard my position, I am at a point where I can identify the source of my problems and attempt to correct them so that my teaching is closer to *my* ideal, *my* expectations—so I will be more satisfied with my performance as a professional." Here she acknowledged that all she really had done in this case investigation was describe her frustration with the district's mandated curriculum; she neither analyzed the "source" of her problems nor made any real attempts to correct them. As her supervisor said, "She's reflecting on the constraints, but she's not reflecting on what she can do about them."

The freewrite for her last case investigation, the lesson case, was directed to her partner, Denys. Carole commented on the lesson she observed him teach and posed several questions to him about what she saw occurring and what it might mean. She raised some important issues but admitted that she really did not know how to interpret what went on: "In terms of structure of lesson—I have no idea how I'll write this paper." Carole had done well at gathering substantial data regarding Denys's lesson; her interviews with Denys and his students and her observation notes for his lesson were thorough and substantial. The readings for the course for which this case investigation was assigned should have provided her with the means for processing that data. However, she was, momentarily at least, stymied by the task of integrating her information into a coherent whole.

This characterization of Carole's thinking processes seems to be borne out by her performance on the case investigations themselves. For two of them she received a score of R on her problem-setting episodes; she was able to set the problem reflectively. However, she was not able to draw reflective conclusions, except in the last case investigation, where she made three generalizations, only one of which was coded as reflective. The teacher case, for instance, was written as she and her supervisor described it: She presented considerable evidence to support the view that the system is very regimented. She also acknowledged her own contribution to her difficulties:

> The situation was not the best of all possible worlds, and a large part of the problem lay in my inability, as I now reflect, to disengage myself from the system. . . . Other experienced Taft teachers

may have found that the only way to deal with the system's lack of time is to double up, to teach two diverse aspects of the English curriculum at once; however, I, as an inexperienced teacher, found the combination to be utterly dissatisfying.

But she did not go on to identify the reasons for her personal difficulties in tackling the situation; nor did she attempt to explore possible solutions by using resources that her supervisor claims were made available to her. She used neither journal data nor observer input in her written analysis.

For the lesson case, Carole again did a thorough job of problem setting. In her teacher interview, she explored and documented the intentions of the teacher and, in fact, seemed to push and to assist him in the clarification of his objectives. The student interviews were also well conducted; she asked multiple, probing questions in casting about for evidence and counterevidence about the lessons learned. The results of these interviews were reported with little unsubstantiated opinion or overgeneralization; thus her problem setting, as exemplified in the following quote, was rated as reflective:

> At no time during my interview with Fred did he mention the words "culture" or "governments" as relating to the quest for the meaning of "West." He entered the classroom with a structure of the concept of "West" based on geography; he left feeling that his structure was inaccurate, but unable to synthesize a structure of "West" in [the teacher's] terms of culture.

Unfortunately, Carole ignored, for the most part, this evidence in her means–ends analysis and conclusions. Even though one of the two students interviewed did understand the concept as intended, Carole concluded that "despite all these positive qualities, Denys failed to reach the objectives of this lesson." This conclusion may have resulted from her own negative reaction to the lesson, as expressed in the observation section of her paper, rather than from the interview data. But these views were mainly unsubstantiated personal opinion: "Indeed, Denys never effectively communicated his desire to avoid geographic boundaries as the only factors involved in defining the West." Such judgments were exactly what the case investigation assignment was trying to counteract.

Carole seemed to be a Commonsense Thinker because when she attempted to interpret data or to formulate generalizations about that data, she had trouble doing so reflectively. She seemed to be "stuck" at the problem-setting stage. It is possible, however, that this "cognitive inability" had emotional roots. Her supervisor mentioned "defensiveness" and "fear"; he pointed out that she was hypercritical of her own performance and that she had a tendency to "play a lot" and to "back away" from difficult tasks. He admitted that he really did not understand why it was so hard for her to apply any of the information in the program to her lesson planning—he did not know whether it was lack of effort, fear of failure, lack of creativity, or something else. Nonetheless, because the nature of Carole's problem seemed to be that she could not carry out the full reflective process, I have categorized her as having problems with the skills of inquiry. This draws attention to the fact that she needed help in the "doing" of reflection.

Paula

Paula's cognitive-processing problems seem to be more extensive; she has trouble engaging in reflective thinking in general. Paula's supervisor gave an indication of this difficulty in his summary evaluation:

> She is a very creative teacher. She often began her senior psychology class with wonderful motivating exercises. Paula's difficulties have come in organizing lectures in a logical fashion or tying together different ideas into one lesson. She is an excellent listener, and does a fine job of incorporating suggestions into her teaching.

Paula's self-assessments tended to corroborate this evaluation of her abilities. On the positive side, she talked in her interviews about how she did try to incorporate the suggestions of her supervisor: "But the great thing is that he has all these suggestions and I think out of everything he's told; me there's always been something that I can use. And so I write it all down and I tell him, 'Okay, I'll do it tomorrow.'" She documented several of these incorporated suggestions, which were in the main logistical in nature: using the final two minutes of class time, drawing up a seating chart, and breaking down large assignments into more manageable pieces. Her discussion of these recommendations did not include any critical analysis of their sources or implications. She did not question why they may have been suggested or pause to consider why or whether she ought to accept them.

Paula frequently mentioned her positive attitude toward the teacher education program and toward the process of learning to teach. She noted that she reads extensively and writes everything down:

> I'm real thorough and I think I've been reading too many books just for every little thing in class. . . . I always take notes and for

me, and I take a lot of notes because when I go back I see the
whole session over again and it just sparks a lot of memories and
that's real valuable. I don't want to leave anything out because
there's always something there—that's my attitude.

She went to considerable lengths to learn from the program, but one of
her reasons for doing so was that she considered herself to be less able
than the other student teachers. Evidence for this appears in her described
response to an instance when her supervisor told her that she was "overdoing it": "I think a lot of it is probably fear or anxiety on my part of
not being up to par with these really, you know, great students or something and so I'm overdoing it." She noted elsewhere that she has "always
known that I require more time studying than a normal person or average
person and I've done that."

Paula also seemed to acknowledge a specific problem with logical
thinking. In her third interview she conversed at length about her reaction
to her supervisor's request that she outline her lectures on the board for
the students. She began by noting with a laugh that she tended to just
"scribble on the board while I talk," which she knew made it hard for the
students to follow. She continued with this explanation:

The thing is that I think I draw—I think in like passage, pathways,
and they have to connect and so even when I'm talking I'm kind of
finding the path that I'm going on. . . . And so it's not like, "Oh,
the map is there." I'm following the cave on my own, even though I
may have thought it through already. So he [her supervisor] said
that maybe, you know, maybe I, he had been pushing and pushing
that I'd come up with these one-liners to put up on the board because I kind of draw on the board and write. And then he said,
then he came up with a really neat idea that maybe I could start in
the middle and kind of start my path. [laughter] Make it at least,
graphically make it understandable, as if it was a spiral or something, which was a lot of help because all of a sudden it made it easier like, "I knew I could think. I know there's something in my
mind, I just can't do this A-B-C outline. . . . But I thought it's important for them [the students] to be able to structure notes the
way they need to and however it's meaningful. But in this book I
need to tell them what to do, what to try to do anyway, and I need
to know what it has to be. That was another problem, organization. So part of it is not knowing what your own thinking pattern
is, you know, and I'm trying to figure it out. And then another one
is, you know, okay, given this, how can it be, how can you make stu-

dents understand it easier? That's something that I'll have to work on for awhile.

This organizational problem is mentioned more than once. Paula referred to her limitations in getting full value from "journal writing" because her way of doing it was often to write little notations of her reactions to different aspects of her experience wherever and whenever those thoughts occurred: "I probably didn't review half my journal because it was scattered all over everything. But I also had organization problems throughout the whole quarter, so, I mean that says a lot."

Paula also noted a need for help in tying ideas together. In her post-study questionnaire she selected a current professor as her best teacher for the following reasons: "He's human and presents his information in a sort of spiral curriculum model. This is great for me because I need to be continually linking things together over and over as we go along." In an interview she critiqued the case investigation assignments by suggesting a need for more direction: "You know, one thing from the class that I think would be helpful for the case study next time is our first freewrite he makes us write, you know, something you taught, what went well, what didn't go well, just a little structuring . . . a few guiding questions."

There is other, less direct evidence in the data of Paula's difficulties with organization and logical thinking. Her interviews were all over the place; she had a tendency to ramble and to free associate. At least three times, she said: "I don't even know if I'm answering the question anymore; you ask me again." She lost sight of the initial focus. She was most tuned in to and distracted by interpersonal relations and dynamics, as is apparent in her response to an interview question about what she notices when she observes another classroom: "I notice students . . . my focus is more what students are doing and how I think the students are reacting to this lesson, and I have real difficulty in noticing the type of lesson that it should be."

None of Paula's cases were scored as reflective. She had particular trouble with problem setting and generalization, which related to her difficulties with making associations, with formulating an integrated picture of a whole situation, idea, or lesson. Only in the lesson case was she able to set a problem reflectively—the case where the nature of the problem and the means for specifying it were detailed. She was never able to draw conclusions reflectively.

Her performance on the student case is an example of this. The question that she chose was too broad and was essentially impossible to answer from a brief case study:

From my observation of and interactions with Celina, it has become apparent to me that she is a caring, sensitive, and extremely
courteous person. Of special interest to me was to what degree, if
any, have Celina's previous educational and/or cultural experiences
contributed to her outlook about people in general, and education
in particular.

As her supervisor responded, "I think everyone's previous experiences
contribute to their present outlook."

In much of her analysis, Paula did not give concrete examples from
the data to support her too firmly stated proposals, for example: "While
living in Mexico, Celina did attend school. She had completed the third
grade when her family moved to the U. S. Thus her writing and reading
skills, in Spanish, were very good." However, she did report some relevant
pieces of data free of interpretation, her only real strength in the case:
"Celina remembers what a struggle it was for her parents to financially
support the family and to keep their children in school. She believes that
even though many people are poor in Mexico, they seem to value their
education more than many American students do." Nonetheless, Paula's
conclusion was not supported by this data, was stated with too much
assurance, and had been derived from an inappropriate and unanswerable
question: "However, I feel it is safe to assume, given her essays, and her
treatment of others that her experiences in Mexico and later as a new
student in American schools, have certainly played a role in creating her
empathy and concern for others."

    The freewrite accompanying this student case pointed toward the
priorities and perspectives that may have interfered with Paula's reflective
thinking. She began with this line: "Writing the case study was not as
great as actually going out and trying to get to know the different Upward
Bound students." She continued with a discussion of how good but ex-
hausting it was to get to know students and how difficult this would be
in her own classes. Then she talked about her concerns with the Upward
Bound program in terms of providing guidance and motivation for minority students and with the inappropriate attitude of some of her peers.
Three-quarters of the way through, she realized she had been distracted.
"Oh yes, about me . . ."—and she made this comment: "I guess I focused
too much on students who were sometimes day dreaming, but the class
must go on." She acknowledged her tendency to overattend to individual
student behavior.

    Paula described herself as a reflective person in the post-study ques-
tionnaire. In her freewrites and her interviews she was supportive of reflection in general and of specific aids to reflection, such as observers and

journals. But her definition of reflection seemed to be similar to sensitivity—thoughtful consideration of others; that is, she understood it more in terms of its human, rather than its substantive aspects, as was typical of her whole approach. She neither saw nor used the process in the systematic way in which I have defined it. Even though the impetus was there, the procedures of problem setting, means–ends analysis, and generalization were difficult for her to carry out on her own. As with Carole, though emotional factors did seem to be in operation, Paula's problems with the processes of reflective thinking made a more significant contribution to her placement as a Commonsense Thinker.

Beth

Beth is the hardest to analyze because she presented so little data. She was the only participant who included no freewrites in the student and teacher case investigations. Both the freewrites for the lesson case were lists of impressions of the lesson observed:

> Shelley accomplished what she planned.
> She was worried about getting student volunteers to interview; but for five points two students agreed.
> The lesson was smooth.
> Students are getting used to doing things differently. This is her fifth day of teaching.
> Good student participation.
> Good ditto to get point across; stresses important things to look for when factoring.

Despite the request for these freewrites to be responses to the exercise of doing the case investigation, Beth did not comment on her own experiences of the process. What she did write were general opinions about the quality of the lesson that were strongly stated and nonanalytical; she raised no issues and asked no questions. This was all the more significant in that it was the first freewrite for this investigation—the one done after the observation of the lesson and prior to the student interviews. The main purpose of this assignment was to analyze the instructional process based on information about what ends up in the minds of learners. Beth did go on to carry out very thorough interviews of two students that were in the main reflectively written, though one discussion had to be rated as indeterminate because she made a definitive statement about the future learning of that student that was not substantiated or justified: "Linda had a good overall understanding of the basic concepts, so consequently she will have no trouble in adding new concepts to the ones she has mastered." Beth did manage to paint a fairly clear picture, well-supported with evidence, of how one student learned and one did not. She said of Josh, for example:

> He was familiar with FOIL and its applications to problems involving trinomials. Josh, however, did not understand the conclusion at the end of the problems in category II. He said that the factors could have two negative signs or just one since the problem had both a positive and negative sign in it. Josh matched up the trinomial with two types of factors when he should have matched it up with category II. He needs to see many examples and draw right conclusions so he can erase his previous misconceptions. He, however, had a very good understanding of the relationship between factors and the trinomial. Josh knew how to fine tune the application of FOIL to multiply $(x + 2)(x + y + 3)$.

Her subsequent analysis, however, treated only the student who learned. In both the case investigation itself and in the accompanying summative freewrite, she completely ignored the fact that one of the students did not learn. She did not try to explain either the difference or the implications of that difference. She did not change her general opinions of the lesson as a result of these interviews. She used the case investigation mainly to compliment the other teacher and to discuss her own previously held views about ways to teach the subject matter of the lesson. There was little analysis or use of the data. The conclusions were statements of her judgment of the content of the lesson without regard to student outcome, speculations about what "the students"[1] would be able to do in the future, and comments on how factoring ought to be taught:

> The students were familiar with multiplication of binomials using the FOIL method. They were then introduced the topic of factoring a binomial and then a trinomial. Thus, the framework for the intended lesson existed and the lesson served as accretion of knowledge for some students. The lesson would help fine tune the concepts and the skills involved in factoring for the students who had done factoring in the past. As students become familiar with the three factoring patterns introduced in the lesson, they will be able to factor with "smoothness" and less "mental effort." Typical problems belonging to any of the three categories will "become automatic" for the students to factor. They will be able to choose appropriate values in their heads to solve problems. The conclusion

drawn at the end of each category will help students to narrow down the possible choices. According to Bruner, students will remember better if they learn by discovery. The handout is carefully designed to lead students to three guided discoveries. Students are more likely to guess the signs in the middle of the factors accurately after the guided discoveries as they take on similar problems in the future.

Learning to factor must use cognitive strategies as domain of learning. A table must be built and appropriate values must be chosen to factor a trinomial. Initially the table of values can be built on paper but eventually students will be able to narrow down the choices and think of appropriate values in their heads. It is very important for students to learn to see the relationships between the signs, the pair of values they choose for the factors and the original trinomial.

Intellectual skills have to be built before students can begin to factor. Associations: students are shown that the sum of three terms are associated with product of two binomials. Discrimination: the nature of factors depends upon the trinomial. Concepts: The concept of factoring is quite difficult to get across. The trinomial essentially is put in another form. This is similar to writing $6 + 4 = 2 \cdot 5$. Rules: There are rules to be followed while factoring and rules to be used to check for accuracy of factors.

Learning to factor definitely involves instrumental and relational understanding.

This was her entire analysis section and the conclusion of her paper, which led the teaching assistant respondent to comment:

Conclusion? You end this paper rather abruptly. Where did this lesson fit into the unit and the course? How did the teacher evaluate student understanding while the lesson was going on? How did she respond to student questions? What was the teacher's reaction to the lesson? You left a lot of unanswered questions.

Beth's teacher case suffered from similar kinds of problems. Her first case investigation, the student case, was the only one in the study with no scorable episodes. She did not do a case investigation at all; she told a story about a student—his escape to freedom, experiences in America, and ambitions for the future. It was a very poignant story but included no questions, no mention of any evidence or data sources, and no analysis, discussion of issues, or conclusions.

Her supervisor's summary evaluation did not discuss her reflectivity. He commended her for her perseverance in tackling a severe classroom control problem, which he attributed to her "lack of experience with the American high school setting." (Beth immigrated to the United States as an adult.)

> She did not have a clear picture (from her own experience) to draw upon. Her lessons were often disorganized and her directions to her students were garbled and often contradictory. This semester, the size of Beth's beginning algebra class was reduced to 13 and Beth gradually began to see a clearer picture of student needs. She continues to have some problems communicating with the lower ability students; she doesn't always follow the students' logic. But there is clearly improvement. Her work in the algebra II class reflected her ability to communicate well with high ability students.

It is possible that her problems in following the logic of lower-ability students and in giving "garbled" and "contradictory" directions were the result of inexperience with American high schools. But difficulties in engaging in the procedures of reflective thinking—problem setting, means–ends analysis, and generalization—may also have been a contributing factor.

The topic of Beth's teacher case was this struggle with classroom management. In the case investigation she posed three possible explanations for her loss of control, but she neither analyzed the sources nor explored the meaning of these possibilities. For instance, her first suggestion was that "though I was given a good idea of the kind of students I would be teaching, the real picture was quite different." She did not discuss what "kind of students" she expected or what she meant by "the real picture." She also did not share what her expectations were, why she held them, or whether they might have been justified. She did not explore any possible relationship among the nature of the students, her expectations, and her classroom control problems. Instead she chronicled her efforts to get the class back after having lost them, for whatever reason. In discussing each of her strategies, she made no reference to input from her observers, did not analyze the possible reasons for what she saw as the success or failure of these attempts, and did not consider the possible implications of the changes made. Her conclusions were platitudes, unconnected to any evidence:

> It is very important to start out on the right foot, especially when culture can be a barrier in communication. It is essential to make

the rules the very first day, be consistent about the rules and from time to time refresh students' memory about the rules. Without the proper environment it is very difficult to get students interested in a subject like mathematics. Management issues should be dealt with immediately and students should be given a chance to get back to the original status without any reference to disruptive behavior. Students may very conveniently forget certain classroom rules. It is essential to stay on top of the situation at all times. It is necessary to be very organized and think the lessons through very thoroughly in terms of details for each of the activities planned and the mechanics of it.

It is possible to get on the right track after not starting out with the right foot, but one should be prepared to stumble many times along the way. The first impression can be very helpful in setting the tone of the class.

When asked in the post-study questionnaire whether the teacher education program encouraged reflection and what reflection meant to her, she responded: "Yes. Look at yourself objectively through the eyes of an observer and be critical." As was typical of Beth's responses, more questions were raised than answered. Did she mean that one cannot reflect on one's own? What do "looking at yourself objectively" and "being critical" entail? It is possible that these words represented for her the process of reflective thinking, as I have defined it. It may be that Beth did engage in reflective thinking that simply was not shared. Nonetheless, the nature of what is missing from the data is significant. When she identified a problem at all, she did not explore its source or meaning. She neither tempered her judgments nor supported them with evidence. Her three cases, all scored as unreflective, included only three reflective episodes. Beth's profound lack of reflective thinking suggests that difficulties with inquiry skills as I have defined them may have been most influential in her being rated as a Commonsense Thinker.

For all cases in this category, the possibility of unshared reflective thinking needs to be considered; one can use an example of reflective thinking to show that someone is capable of it, but one cannot use an absence of reflective thinking to show that she is not. As Kitchener (1986) advises, distinctions need to be made between reflective ability and verbal ability. Perhaps Carole, Paula, and Beth were simply not as open or as eloquent about their thought processes as were the others. But evidence in this study tends to minimize that possibility. First, it is not just that reflective thinking was absent; faulty reasoning processes were present.

Second, although there were no taciturn yet reflective participants, there were examples of unreflective "chattiness." Paula, for instance, tended to expound at length in response to her interview questions but was seldom analytical or reflective. Heather, an Alert Novice, wrote two lengthy and eloquent cases that were not rated as reflective. Third, and most important, the participants were placed in the Alert Novice or Commonsense Thinker categories on the basis of their pre-study questionnaire responses, not their performance on the cases. The questions used in the final scoring system were selected in part because of their comparability in terms of style and length. That is, the responses given by all the student teachers to the questions used for subject identification were similar in length and coherence; there were no great differences in terms of expressive ability.

A relevant problem for this and future studies is that the cognitive requirements of reflective thinking have yet to be well defined. As Gardner (1983) observes, neither specific intelligences nor more general synthesizing mechanisms have been adequately formulated or explained. Thus they are difficult to detect and to evaluate. But, as I argue in Chapter 1, some form of intelligent functioning seems to be a necessary, though not sufficient, component of reflective thinking, and thus should be considered in our conceptions of and designs for reflective teacher education, especially since research indicates that many beginning teachers may need assistance in these areas (Feiman-Nemser & Buchmann, 1987; Lanier & Little, 1986; Reyes, 1987; Schlechty & Vance, 1983; Vance & Schlechty, 1982). The cases of Carole, Paula, and Beth lend support to this position. These results suggest that we need to direct our efforts to the definition, diagnosis, and remediation of inquiry skills; but in doing so, we must be cautious about inferring inability from an absence of reflective thinking. Even more important, we must guard against assuming reflective ability from eloquence, because if reflectivity is in fact not present, it may remain undeveloped due to oversight. Taking a close look at the thought processes of novices such as Carole, Paula, and Beth will contribute to this endeavor.

EMOTIONAL INTERFERENCE

The other three students in the Commonsense Thinker category were Geoff, Rachel, and Andrea. In contrast to Carole, Paula, and Beth, who produced no reflective cases, each of these participants produced at least one reflective case—Andrea produced two. These individuals were capable of reflective thinking but did not do so as consistently as Alert Novices. Most critically, they were not likely to be "spontaneously reflective," due to the distraction or constraint of emotions or attitudinal perspectives. They may have had minimal internal impetus for making the effort necessary to engage in reflective thinking. They were Commonsense Thinkers because they tended not to reflect, even though they had the cognitive skills to do so. Again, the specific nature of the interference varied for the three individuals in this subcategory.

Geoff

Geoff seemed to be overconfident and rather unmotivated. One of his two supervisors described him this way:

> I think he was a little on the "how little can I do to get by" type. I think he felt he was doing a good job in the classroom and cared about his students. I don't think he was as committed to his coursework at [the university] as a number of his colleagues. He was self-confident and yet wanted feedback on how he was doing in his classes. As a reflective teacher I wouldn't put him at the top of the scale but he did think about his classroom practice and students.

This sense of self-confidence was apparent in his pre-study questionnaire. In response to a question about why he wanted to teach, he stated, "Because I know I can be a very good teacher and I would enjoy teaching. I also believe there is a need for me as a teacher at the high school level." This self-assurance appeared again in his post-study questionnaire response to the same question: "I want to teach because I'm good at it and I will make a positive difference in kids' lives." Nonetheless, he did express some concerns when he talked in his pre-study questionnaire about what he thought teaching would be like:

> Teaching in a classroom will be nerve racking. I'll be sweating. I'll be worried whether or not they're listening. If they're listening, I'll be worried whether or not they're understanding. If they're understanding, I'll worry whether or not they'll remember it tomorrow. I hope they'll respect me as a teacher *and* as a person. It will be a very demanding role and I look forward to the challenge.

Self-confidence is, of course, not a bad thing; in fact, it would be nice if more beginning teachers had more of it. An attitude like that expressed above could serve them well in facing the considerable challenges of the teaching profession. Problems with self-assurance arise only when it interferes with an orientation toward growth and development. Bolin (1987) makes such an observation in his case study of Lou, a preservice science teacher: "In many respects, teaching is easy for Lou. This may work against his growth as a deliberative teacher because he is satisfied. There is no compelling reason to reflect" (p. 6). Lou's supervisor noted that "he is very thorough about method and technique in teaching, often asking . . . for ideas. He is less thoughtful about the principles behind method or technique, however" (p. 7). This description is reminiscent of the evaluation by Geoff's supervisor. Bolin suggests that this superficial treatment of problems may be partly due to complacency.

Evidence in the data suggests that Geoff, like Lou, was not as deeply reflective as he could be and that one cause may have been a lack of perceived need. His student case was extremely unreflective, more so than any other in the study (except for Beth's student case, which was not a case investigation at all), with no reflective episodes and 94% unreflective episodes. The case investigation was rampant with stereotypes, overgeneralizations, and overassurances. The problem was stated in a way that almost precluded a thorough investigation: "Does John's Mexican heritage prevent him from succeeding in school in particular and in America in general?" Geoff did conclude with a "resounding 'no,'" but on the basis of the argument that students of color do not require and should not request any differential treatment; as long as they are able to adopt the dominant culture and be "typical teenagers," they will do fine in school and in life. Geoff failed to explore the implications or meanings of his terms and conclusions. He oversimplified the issues and thus failed to explore the problem in any depth or with any accuracy. He raised no questions about the inequities of the system or the society into which he suggested John had assimilated, and he did not consider what the negative implications of such an assimilation might be. The following citations are illustrative of his approach:

> Living in what I suspect is a mostly Hispanic community, John was never made to feel out of place as he was growing up. Even if his older brothers didn't carve a niche within the community, John's background was so typical of the neighborhood that there is no reason to believe that he should have been struggling to fit into American society. . . .
>
> John is in every way a normal, American boy (if indeed such a child exists). In fact he is probably more "normal" than most Americans of American descent.

Geoff was certain about the conclusions he reached concerning John—a "resounding 'no'" and "there is no doubt that John will succeed in life."

This attitude was supported in the accompanying freewrite, which continued to build upon these judgments:

> Having had only limited experience working with minorities, I cherished the chance to explore their sensitivities. I wasn't sure at first if my questions would be insulting, or even if they were relevant. What I discovered is that minorities, at least the ones I talked to, are not ashamed of being minorities (not that they should be). Yes, many Hispanics speak Spanish, so asking about Spanish is an appropriate question. However, I would still avoid questioning that denies or confirms stereotypes. (For example, asking Blacks if they like watermelon.)
>
> The case study forced me to think about the practical side of minorities in the classroom. I stick to my previous belief that all students have an equal capacity for learning. If, by chance, a student has a language problem or a deficiency in fundamental skills, then certainly these needs must be addressed. However, they must be addressed as if it was a member of the dominant group that had these weaknesses.

Geoff admitted that his previous beliefs, though derived from limited experience with minorities, had remained unchanged by the experience. His initial certainties may have helped to prevent the reflective exploration necessary to the restructuring of misconceptions.

Geoff's lesson case was more reflective, but still quite mixed; episodes from all three stages of the reflective process were split between reflective and unreflective scores, which was not true of any other case in the study. He continued to have a problem with overgeneralization: "From what I could tell the class as a whole seemed to be understanding everything." He did, however, go to great lengths to define the nature of the problem—in this case to determine student learning from an interview process. He devoted five different episodes to this determination, more than any other author of the lesson cases. His conclusion also had four episodes, half rated as unreflective and half as reflective. The reflective features of the conclusion were that he acknowledged some surprises, applied the course readings well (which he did not do elsewhere in the case investigation), and posed some tentative generalizations that followed appropriately from the means–ends analysis:

> As David demonstrated, one can be quiet and still not pay attention. On the other hand, Laura demonstrated that one can pay attention and still not get the right message. What went wrong? The most tempting thing to do is shrug our collective shoulders and de-

clare that some students just aren't suited for learning some subjects. What easier way to explain the fact that some students
learned the material and others did not? Truly, such responses don't
answer the questions, they only avoid them. According to Bruner,
"any subject can be taught effectively in some intellectually honest
form to any child at any stage of development." The problem is not
the learner nor the subject. It is the form. The form [the teacher]
used was fine for him and me, but not for all of the students.

The unreflective features of his conclusion had to do with a tendency
to oversimplify the problem. He implied, for example, that the main solution to the question of student learning was for students to pay attention
better and become more "sophisticated learners" who could "separate
tangents from the main circle of topics." He left many aspects of the
teacher's actual presentation out of his analysis, which may in part be
accounted for by his approach to the assignment, as portrayed in the accompanying freewrite: "Alas, it seems the fun never ends. My enthusiasm
for this assignment has waned considerably as I undertake each new step.
Lord knows what'll happen when it's time to write the paper." He talked
about the problems he and his partner had in staying on topic in their
conversations both after the lesson observation and after the student interviews as well as about their difficulties in interpreting the meaning of
the data they had gathered: "My partner and I began this interview with
very little to say. Although we identified a few gaps in the students' learning, we were more inclined to throw up our hands than dig deeply into
the underlying reasons." He then posed questions about why the students
did not learn from the physics lesson in the same way that he did, an issue
also presented in the final case investigation write-up. In both instances
there was some, but not enough, acknowledgment of why this might have
been an inappropriate comparison. The comparison was to be between
the intended objectives and the outcomes for the two students, not between the learning of the students and the learning of the observer—who
was not only an adult, a former engineer, and a math–science teacher, but
also an individual already informed about the purpose and content of
the lesson.
     The one reflective case investigation that Geoff produced was the
teacher case. In it he set an appropriate case investigation problem: He
attempted to discover why the students in his geometry class had become
bored. This situation had come as a real shock to Geoff:

When I realized that such behavior was occurring with regularity, I
was frightened. Not by my students (I'm much bigger than they),

but by myself. You see, I had this vision of myself as one of the best teachers ever to step . . . into a classroom. Overqualified, bursting with social skills, everybody's friend. They would think of me, I dreamed, as the solution to education's problems. Concepts that were thought to be difficult would be suddenly elucidated by my witty analogies and logical problem solving. I would never have any management problems because everyone in my class would be too interested in learning to think about doing anything else. But the amazing thing . . . is that I was right, to a degree. Things were going just as I had planned . . . . Just why things were going so great I never bothered to inquire. I figured that my earlier expectations were correct and that indeed the proper education of future generations was ensured. It wasn't until things weren't so rosy that I started asking questions. And that was when the fear hit. The fear of being average. I didn't quit my job as an engineer to be an average teacher. I was determined to be good. Really good. There are many reasons that I could accept for not succeeding as a teacher. But my own mediocrity was not one of them. To avoid being "just another teacher," I determined to identify whatever reasons I could to explain the change in my geometry students' attitude and behavior.

Geoff granted that he was confident that things would go well for him; he also noted that he was not inclined to reflect when things were going as expected. He was forced into reflection only when there was a perceived discrepancy between those expectations and reality. When this situation arose, he was able to carry out the process fairly successfully. Although he still had a tendency to oversimplify and overgeneralize with too much certainty—"And the reasons for this are quite clear"—he did document well his definition of the problem and its development. He acknowledged the role of his supervisor in recognizing the problem and posed several possible explanations for why it arose. He explored a number of solutions and, in doing so, incorporated some lessons from the teacher education program. However, in evaluating these efforts, his judgments were based mainly on "what works" without much in-depth exploration of the reasons why or why not, a problem that will be discussed further in Chapter 5.

In the associated freewrite for this case, Geoff denied much of the value of the reflective process in which he had engaged:

I think doing a case study on one's self is an excellent idea, although I'm not sure that the particular format that was set up is particularly useful or enlightening. All the things I said above are true. My class was boring and it took me awhile to realize it. But it's tough. Geometry is not the easiest subject in the world to teach. There are no movies you can show, debates to set up, or lively discussion on the impact of geometry on world peace. To a math teacher geometry is intrinsically interesting, but to the student that got a D in algebra I, it is not. Some things work and some things don't, but believe me I'll try anything once (sometimes twice); even I get bored sometimes.

He tended to claim that he did not learn anything new from the case investigation and that the problem was almost unresolvable anyway: Geometry is boring—period.

Geoff was a Commonsense Thinker mainly because of his attitude: He was more unwilling to reflect than he was unable. He never really became convinced of the need to reflect, but when the assignment was structured so that he had to, as in the teacher and the lesson cases, he begrudgingly did so, at least to a point. He seemed to be somewhat over-confident about his abilities, which reduced his willingness to make the considerable effort required for reflective thinking and productive change. He continued to hold several stereotypes of students that were also a hindrance, which was quite evident in the student case and its free-write. Overgeneralizations also appeared in a post-study questionnaire response—"Some students will learn no matter how poorly you teach and some will never learn despite your best efforts"—and in one statement in his teacher case—"Oh, of course there were the stupid students who would just never understand, but by and large my students liked geometry." This perspective did not provide much incentive for reflection in teaching. Nor did it allow for critical reflection on the social and moral implications of his ideas and practices.

Geoff did see the benefit in looking back over experiences, as this quote from the teacher case demonstrates: "However, it would have been even worse of a failure if I hadn't done the careful evaluation that identified what went wrong." But his judgment of how this process functions was oversimplistic: "I always try something. At least then I know. And if I do a good job of self-evaluation, then I know what to do to make it better." His confidence in his own teaching, justified or not, and his stereotypical overgeneralizations about students did not provide the internal impetus necessary for undertaking more than a surface-level exploration of problems. When an external event created a significant discrepancy between his beliefs or expectations and his experience, however, he was able to carry out an act of reflection.

Rachel

Rachel was also capable of reflection, as her performance on the student case demonstrated. Her placement in the Commonsense Thinker category derived from her tendency to become overwhelmed and distracted by the disparate requirements of her life. Her supervisor's summary evaluation, though highly complimentary, expressed concern about the potential repercussions of her tendency to overextend:

> Do I have a favorite student? Yes, Rachel. I worried at first whether she could do it all: no money (had to moonlight); crazy and intense by nature; boyfriend, up again down again; and constantly doing more in classroom prep than any superhuman could stand. And yet, she was a true and thorough success story. Kids love her. Peers and supervisors acknowledge her warmth and intensity (in a positive sense). She is bright, chipper and complete; and if she doesn't fall emotionally over the next few years, she'll become a great teacher. I do worry that Rachel will take on too much, that she might not seek help or support when she needs assistance.

Rachel's performance in her case investigations, particularly her teacher and lesson cases, did give indications of scattered thinking and distractibility. In her teacher case, which was scored as indeterminate, Rachel did not actually set a problem at all. She reported on a conversation that she had had with a friend the night before writing the paper (and subsequent to a computer crash in which she had lost a nearly complete first draft). Rachel's friend was a resident adviser for one of the campus houses who was frustrated with the "general lack of interest" and sense of shared responsibility on the part of the residents. In the course of this conversation, Rachel was "struck by the similarities between her [friend's] role as resident adviser" and her own as teacher:

> The concerns she was voicing were concerns I had grappled with at the beginning of my teaching career and am still concerned with. How do you "hook" your students or your fellow house members? How do you facilitate their understanding of a problem? How do you involve them in activities so that "ownership" is achieved? How do you separate yourself from volatile situations or issues and act as a responsible and fair facilitator of discussion? How do you get your students or house members to start from the beginning of an argument which you have already been deliberating for days on and have reached your own conclusions about? And without presenting a biased viewpoint?

Rachel gave some advice to her friend and in doing so realized "how much I really have learned and do know about what I consider to be the most important facet of teaching—the process of learning."

The situation described is almost an "ideal" reflective setting: An external impetus caused Rachel to raise some important questions and to surface and share some implicit educational beliefs. Where, then, was the difficulty? Why was the case rated as indeterminate? The main problem was that Rachel seemed to confuse two terms; she moved back and forth between a discussion of "the process of learning" and the context for learning without acknowledging or defining the differences or the relationship. Rachel never made it clear that the aim of her friend was "learning" in the same sense as classroom learning. The house adviser wanted participation, interest, commitment, and shared responsibility more than she wanted "learning." Rachel did make some good suggestions to her friend, but again these suggestions had more to do with how to motivate and create ownership among colleagues than with the process of learning. At any rate, these suggestions were not critically analyzed, nor were they backed by any evidence or theory. What follows is an example of two of her suggestions:

> I suggested having different people in the house being assigned one
> item from the agenda as theirs to facilitate. In that way, maybe
> there would be more input from the house members themselves and
> thus more interest in meetings. I suggested making up question-
> naires to be passed out to each house member before a meeting and
> filled out anonymously so that my friend or someone else in the
> house could compile a list of responses for house discussion before
> it even began. In this way, house members would have the chance to
> think about issues before the meeting and present their ideas so
> that the meeting could be more productive when everyone gathered
> together.

The right atmosphere does need to be established in order for learning to take place, but it is not the same as the learning process. If Rachel had simply been mislabeling—if she had actually been talking about motivation and was just calling it the learning process—then the problem may not have been so significant. However, in another section of the case investigation, where she talked specifically about her beliefs about learning, she did seem to be referring to the actual learning process: "So what was it that made them truly excellent teachers? It was the fact that every one of these teachers possessed the ability to present the material from a perspective which all the students could understand and then work with the students until they reached a more refined analytical understanding of the subject matter." In the course of this discussion, she made another observation about effective teaching that was based on her personal experience as a learner. She did not temper it by noting that what "worked" for her may not work for everyone.

Rachel did acknowledge in her conclusion, which was supported in the accompanying freewrite, that she needed to continue to think about the issue:

> I don't know how it will go for my friend, but I do know that our conversation really instilled in me a knowledge of what I have learned through [the program] and my teaching experience. It also gave me an understanding about all I do know about the process of teaching. I still have a long way to go but I feel that I am on the right track. If I can continue to implement the idea of giving my students the tools by which they can understand whatever subject I am teaching, then I feel that I am being a good teacher. For then my students can use those tools to learn anything they want or need to learn for the rest of their lives.

The conclusion was appropriately tempered, but it contained some further variation of terms. Here she mentioned the "process of teaching" rather than learning and made reference to means for helping students learn how to learn. Rachel never clarified what exactly she was reflecting upon.

Rachel's lesson case was even more problematic in this regard. In essence, she carried out an entirely different task than the one intended. She interviewed the students about pedagogy rather than content. She talked to them about, and thus based her case analysis on, their understanding and appreciation of the teaching techniques rather than the substance of the lesson, as is evident in her list of student interview questions:

1. What did you perceive were the objective(s) of the lesson?
2. How do you learn things?
3. What does this teacher do to help you learn things?
4. How do you feel about memorizing?
5. Do you have problems with the amount of material covered?
6. Do you feel that there are special management concerns in this class?
7. Do you feel that there are problems with the small group work in this class?

She never determined whether the students learned the content the teacher intended to convey; indeed, she did not even discuss this issue. So again, though some reflection occurred in the case, it was all in the first two sections of the write-up, which, in this case, involved only data-gathering that was unrelated and prior to problem definition and analysis. Her whole approach to problem definition, analysis, and conclusion was thus unreflective because it was based on a faulty conception of the task.

Rachel was capable of reflection. She also seemed to favor the process, although the evidence for this is minimal. She did not, for instance, respond to the post-study questionnaire question, "What does it mean to you to be a reflective teacher?" As mentioned above, her teacher freewrite did indicate a desire and a need to continue "thinking and rethinking" about the issue "for the rest of her teaching career." In her lesson case freewrites for her partner she talked about the importance of asking her students for feedback and about the value of having talked with a partner before and after a lesson:

> Talking . . . really made me seriously consider my objectives and reasons for teaching the lesson; it also helped me think and rethink why I was doing what I wanted to do and how I might implement some of the ideas that came up . . . although the exercise took a lot of time, it was useful to bounce off ideas on a new audience and get responses. Well worth it!

Rachel seemed to be a Commonsense Thinker not because she was deficient in inquiry skills, nor because she saw no need for reflection, but rather because she tended to get distracted by a detail that might distort the "big picture." She tended to focus on one representation of the issue and fail to attend to other aspects of the idea or situation. In her teacher case she talked about "hooking" house members instead of the process of learning. In the lesson case she discussed the learners perception of the teacher's pedagogical techniques rather than the content of the lesson. These examples suggest that the factors she tended to focus on or be distracted by were those related to general pedagogy. Her pre-study questionnaire contains some evidence to support this suggestion. She mentioned her fears of speaking in front of groups of students, and when asked to take the perspective of the students in the videotape, did not do so. Instead she critiqued the teacher from her own perspective, focusing on how well she thought the students responded to him. Although general pedagogical techniques are an important topic for reflection, they should not be the only topic. More important, Rachel's problem was not so much that she dealt only with such issues, but that these issues tended to take over and become confused with other ideas under consideration. The reason for this is difficult to determine from the data. I have suggested that an explanation worth pursuing is the interference of disruptive emotions; her worry over personal concerns may not only muddle her thinking but also make practical issues seem more pressing.

Andrea

Andrea's problem was easier to detect: She was suffering from a severe lack of self-confidence. Her supervisor said this of her in his summary evaluation:

> When I first started working with Andrea in the summer of 19____ she was extremely motivated to become the best teacher she could. She felt inadequately prepared in her subject area (which she was but not to the extent she perceived this as an inadequacy). The lack of self-confidence was the trait that stands out in my mind when I think about Andrea. She could not accept herself as being as good as her peers and they even commented on her negative self-perception during the days she taught the Upward Bound class. Andrea was very open-minded and her desire to improve was evident in the changes she made in her teaching. The end result was not in her lack of desire for change but all the other shortcomings and as Bandura would say low level of self-efficacy. Andrea never really felt confident in her ability to achieve her own model of what a good teacher is. This I believe gave her a very slim chance of feeling successful and therefore she was going to fail. As a reflective individual I think she would be high on a scale because she never thought what she would do could be the best way.

Other data seem to corroborate the supervisor's assessment of Andrea. Substantial evidence to support the notion that she had a low self-image will be referred to throughout this discussion, but it is most apparent in a quotation from Andrea's teacher case, where she described the same events in similar terms:

> My low self-perception is not a new problem. My demeanor during the summer had been very somber. When I was videotaped, the entire intern class saw how I was very self-critical. For example, several people noticed that I did not smile the entire three days I taught. However, most people noticed how I belittled myself in front of my Upward Bound students for not sticking to the class

schedule of activities. I know it was not a big deal, but I wanted everything to be perfect. Consequently, I proceeded to chastise myself every time I perceived something had gone wrong. I felt inadequate because I could not live up to my "mind's eye" model of how a teacher should act. Although most of the interns told me to "lighten up," this comment fell on deaf ears.

The statement also acknowledges the discrepancy her supervisor mentioned between her idea of what teaching ought to be and what she saw it to be in practice.

Nonetheless, Andrea, as her supervisor also suggested, was capable of reflection. In fact, her teacher case was one of the most reflective in the study; all of the episodes were scored as reflective. This case investigation required her to focus on a personal issue, and the issue that she chose was her lack of self-confidence and its negative impact on her classroom. She made a very real effort to understand the reasons behind the extreme classroom management problems she was experiencing. Her emotional reactions to the situation were exacerbated by the fact that these difficulties so challenged the aforementioned image of herself in the teaching role. This image of herself was also apparent in her pre-study questionnaire. When responding to the question about what it would be like to be a teacher in the classroom, she stated, "It will feel comfortable; like being at home. I know I will radiate a kind of aura that the kids will pick up that says subconsciously to them 'I care and I want to be here for you as a teacher and a model.'" Elsewhere she stated that "I feel teaching comes natural to me. I feel I have a certain style when I enter the classroom, i.e., I really come alive."

Survival was the issue for Andrea, and she went to great pains to explore and be thoughtful about the sources of her unexpected and extreme difficulties. As a result, she gained insight into herself and her teaching that she had not had before: "Unfortunately, the most destructive aspect of my low self-concept is my negative attitude towards my class. I was completely unaware of this until I had a fellow student teacher observe my class." She followed this statement with a thorough documentation of the debriefing between herself and this observer:

> During the debriefing, I told my peer to have sympathy on me for having such a crummy group of kids who were hyperactive. He turned to me and said: "Andrea, you are so negative. No one in your room is getting any positive reinforcement from you for the good behaviors some of your kids are doing. You are so hung up with the few kids that aren't listening, etc. that you can't see the

ones who are obeying you. Believe me, there are kids in your class who want to learn." I was stymied by that remark. I didn't believe him.

She continued with more examples of her observer's efforts to "open her eyes." He told her about an incident in which she reprimanded the whole class because one student did not have the spiral notebook she had asked them to bring. He pointed out to her that "half the class held up their spiral notebooks. . . . However, you didn't see it. You were too busy seeing the kids who didn't have their notebooks." At the end she commented:

> While my peer was relating this story to me, I could remember Melanie with a big smile on her face waving her spiral notebook in front of me saying: "See, Miss _____, I even have yesterday's assignment in it." I just stood there and ignored her and everyone else who was eagerly showing me that they had complied with my request for spiral notebooks. It was finally starting to sink in what my observer was trying to impress upon me.

This realization sent her to the literature (something no one else in the study did) to "see if there was any scientific validity to what my fellow student was saying about teacher self-concept and classroom management." So keen was her interest in finding answers that she read seven different articles on the topic.

In the course of doing this reflective investigation, Andrea came to understand the sources of her difficulties. However, she also began to recognize the complexity and enormity of the efforts involved in making the necessary changes. She realized that for her to become the effective teacher she wanted to be, she would have to make some significant changes in her personality. She ended her case with this poignant and telling statement:

> I wish I could end my case study by saying that I am now a person who sees "stars"[2]—a teacher automatically using positive reinforcement daily and having no classroom management problems. But, I am still a person who sees "bars"—a teacher sporadically using positive reinforcement and having many classroom management problems. However, when my metamorphosis is complete some day and I become a teacher who sees "stars," I know that personally and professionally I will have made great strides. At times, I feel like the task of restructuring my thought process is too great a challenge for me to take on but I try to remember—"the longest journey begins with a single step."

This case investigation shows that Andrea was capable of reflection, but it also shows that her self-concept and idealism got in the way of her being able to reflect about students or instructional processes. She was incapable of stepping back from the situation enough to determine what was actually occurring and to think about that productively. She could not "see," and thus could not process, Melanie and her notebook until an outside observer forced her to do so.

The same sort of interference appeared in her student case, which was rated as unreflective. This was a very short, superficial case investigation about "why Jim slept through a large proportion of the 'Investigations in Science' class." She listed a number of possible explanations but did not explain the selection or order of the alternatives. She reported her one interview with the student verbatim, but very little of it had anything to do with her research question. She never asked Jim some obvious questions, such as "Why are you so tired in class?" or "What time do you go to bed at night?" or "Do you like the 'Investigations in Science' course?" She did not appear to have taken the assignment too seriously.

The freewrite for this case investigation (quoted in its entirety in Chapter 3) indicates that her negative self-concept, particularly as it relates to her identification with her case investigation student, may have interfered with the reflective process:

> I had basically given it up for lost that I was going to learn a lot about my student. However, I then began to reflect upon the feelings this student was evoking in me. These feelings were deep inadequacies in my own personality. I wanted to be outgoing, I want to be witty, and I wanted to be popular. Myself and my student were more alike than different and I disliked the parts of me I saw in him. I think this is a valuable insight to my psychological make-up and now that I have this awareness, I will be able to slowly take steps to change myself into a person I like better. In doing this, I will become a more effective teacher.

When Andrea's identity as a person or as a teacher was threatened, which occurred frequently because her self-concept was so fragile, she was unable to be reflective.

In the lesson case, where the subject under investigation was another teacher and where that individual did not trigger any emotional identification, Andrea was able to be reflective. In the freewrites accompanying this case, she did not refer to herself at all. But in the companion paper, which involved a fellow student's observations of her teaching (the same one who was her observer for the teacher case), she again used her freewrite to comment about her personal struggles as a teacher. She wrote a page and a half to him about her reactions to her own lesson, with some positive and some negative comments. In it she attempted to analyze what went well and what did not, why, and what she could have done differently. But then at the end she switched to a negative reaction to her ongoing classroom management problems and wrote another page that foreshadowed her eventual decision not to enter teaching:

> My classroom management sucks. Sometimes I feel sorry for the kids who really want to learn because they must tolerate the "wild bunch." Science is life and technology. I view the teaching of science as a means to obtain knowledge about the methods and technology of maintaining a balance between man and his environment. Besides, Denys, I had this unrealistic dream that I could be creative and really make science come alive for the kids. I used to be very creative in teaching nutrition concepts to little kids and I really had a flare for presentations at Berkeley to grad students. Obviously, I made a mistake about my ability to work with adolescents. We just aren't making the link. I come off as either a pansy or a bitch. I wanted to make a difference because I am really a caring person but I am finding out "caring" isn't enough. My subject matter is too weak and my kids and I are in constant power struggles. Don't worry, I will find my spot in life.

Through this very painful process of reflection upon herself and her teaching, Andrea came to better understand herself and the sources of her problems. She also gradually realized that the nature and degree of her difficulties were not conducive to good teaching and that she should not teach, at least until the problems are resolved, an assessment with which her supervisor agreed. For some individuals such a conclusion may be a productive outcome of reflection in teacher education.

Andrea was a Commonsense Thinker because her self-image interfered with her ability to develop realistic expectations for her own teaching, as her naive responses to the pre-study questionnaire indicate (the responses that formulated the basis of her placement in this category). Her negative self-concept also made it difficult for her to distance herself from the students and the teaching situation enough to allow for appropriate observation, analysis, or judgment.

For Geoff, Rachel, and Andrea, emotions and attitudinal perspectives seemed to prevent or to distort the reflective process they had the ability to perform. As Anzul and Ely (1988) note, efforts to promote reflection may fail for some students: "They may be those who choose not to open up, those for whom reflection is too painful or too threatening, those who believe either that they are already sufficiently aware or that such awareness is not particularly useful" (p. 678). Calderhead (1989) makes a similar observation when he suggests the following:

> The process of learning to teach would seem to be influenced by certain attitudes and metacognitive skills (ways of thinking about learning) which do not appear to be developed easily. Some student teachers, for instance, seem to have great difficulty acquiring the detachment from their own practice that enables them to reflect upon it critically and objectively. (p. 47)

Schön (1988) emphasizes the fact that reflective teaching "takes self-confidence and support" because it "opens a teacher to confusion, to not-knowing, hence to vulnerability" (p. 23). Fuller and Bown (1975), who characterize teaching in general as "constant, unremitting self-confrontation" (p. 48), go on to say:

> From such a process are saints—and blind men—made. Class "control" is difficult because feedback about herself is impossible for a teacher to deny. Pupils tacitly, if not overtly, let the teacher know what they think, what they learn, how they feel about her. Learning to tolerate, nay to seek systematically, to assess, perceive, and use such information, is the sine qua non of teaching. But truthful feedback can be excruciating. (p. 48)

Those most likely to develop into "blind men" may be those for whom the process is too painful, too time-consuming and overwhelming, or just not important enough. Inquiry skills are not sufficient to the task. As emotion theory and research suggests, an appropriate emotional state may be necessary to motivate the engagement of the cognitive processes. In Izard's (1977) words:

> Emotion and cognition are sometimes contrapuntal—they may be in opposition or in harmony. In either case emotion alters perception and cognition. It is proposed that certain emotion states deautomatize or otherwise alter the structures and contents of consciousness in such a way as to preclude cognitive processes as they usually operate. (p. 157)

Emotions influence both the selection and the interpretation of data. "Experiential affect provides the ongoing motivational state that modifies, controls, and directs behavior moment by moment" (Izard, 1977, p. 3). The cases of Geoff, Rachel, and Andrea seem to be indicative of such an association between cognition and emotion. These results suggest that emotions and attitudes play an important role in the process of reflection.

But emotions are not necessarily a negative influence. As Peters (1969) put it, "Emotions are intimately and properly connected with judgments about certain typical objects or situations" (p. 374). They may detract from performance or enhance it, but in any event understanding of emotions is essential to understanding of behavior:

> Unless one knows what a person has "in mind," how he appraised a situation, what information about it he is employing, it is impossible to know what type of "behavior" is being studied. There is all the difference between one's arm being raised and raising one's arm. (Peters, 1969, p. 392)

Izard (1977), in discussing the work of Sinnott (1966), notes that he also emphasizes "the importance of affective experience even in the business of achieving understanding and knowledge. . . . Sinnott remarked that the biologist studying life objectively from an external standpoint may never understand it as well as the poet who can *feel* what it is like" (p. 140). In the next chapter I will discuss how the positive attitudes and emotions of the Alert Novices appear to augment the reflective process.

CONCLUSION

Goodman (1991) has observed that each semester he has a few students in his course "who only marginally complete their unit assignments due to a lack of interest, motivation or intellectual ability" (p. 73). He doubts that these individuals will ever assume the role of moral craftsperson. The performances of the six Commonsense Thinkers in this study create similar misgivings. However, the separate case studies do suggest ways in which we might modify interventions with such students in order to enhance their possibilities for growth, suggestions to be discussed at length in Chapter 6.

What is particularly noteworthy is how different the problems seem to be for each individual and how those variations seem to call for very different forms of assistance. Carole, for instance, had some real strengths of observation and analysis, but she bogged down when it came to formulating possible solutions to the problems she had identified. She is reminiscent of the student teachers described by Britzman (1986) who find themselves in "involuntary collusion with authoritarian pedagogy" (p. 454). Knowing more what not to do than what to do, they see no way of changing their frustrating situations. Though Carole's supervisor did believe she was provided with much help in envisioning alternatives, perhaps this information nccdcd to be offered to her in a different form. Maybe, as Liston and Zeichner (1990) propose, her own educational values and beliefs needed to be made more explicit. Perhaps she might have engaged in an action research project in which she had to develop and test various solutions to her problems. What seemed to be called for in Carole's case was some concentrated assistance in the synthesizing of information from a variety of sources into a new perspective and plan of action.

Paula's difficulties, on the other hand, raise an entirely different set of issues. She was a very creative individual with real empathy and concern for students as people. She had her own way of processing information—more intuitive than logical—that had been quite successful for her. Perhaps rather than trying to get Paula to become more logical, her instructors might have tried to help her understand, value, and better operationalize her own ways of thinking. For instance, instead of asking her to structure the notes she wrote on the board better, she might have been encouraged to create cooperative group discovery lessons, which do not require the linear presentation of information. She seemed to need help in developing a way to analyze and present material to students that is more true to her nature while at the same time building ways to extend, complement, and critically reflect upon that nature.

Kagan (1992) raises questions about timing in teacher education: "Whether a novice is able to accomplish this [reconstruction of prior images] also appears to depend on the novice's biography—particularly whether he or she has reached the point in life where dysfunctional beliefs can be acknowledged and altered" (p. 142). This issue seems relevant to the three Commonsense Thinkers with emotional interferences. Andrea decided for herself that she had not reached a point in her life when her dysfunctional beliefs could be altered. That conclusion does not seem appropriate for Rachel, however, whose difficulties were less profound. She seemed more distracted (especially from her course assignments, including the case investigations) than deeply disturbed. It seems possible in her case that the new ideas and approaches being presented to her were not passing her by; she may have been learning reflective processes that she will be able to operationalize at some later time in her life. How such delayed reaction might be facilitated would be an important programmatic issue in the education of Rachel.

The cases of the six Commonsense Thinkers emphasize the need for a degree of individualized instruction in teacher education. It is not enough to design generic strategies for encouraging reflective activity and

growth, especially with those who most need assistance. Particular intellectual, attitudinal, and emotional states, traits, and abilities must be considered and addressed. The cases of the six Alert Novices reported in the
next chapter offer additional ideas for the form and direction of such interventions.

5

The Alert Novices

*If I ever think that I know what I'm doing is right, I really want to
step back and check my premise.*

(Denys)

In examining the case studies of the six Alert Novices, certain characteristic thought processes seemed to emerge as distinctive of the group as a whole: the tendency to be guided by a strong belief, or "passionate creed," and the propensity for asking "why" questions. In contrast to the Commonsense Thinkers, this group did not break down into subgroups; they all had these qualities in varying degrees. But the power of these two features is not limited to their use in the identification of Alert Novices. The structure and influence of the passionate creeds and the "why" questions are also helpful in explaining differences in the individual performances of all participants. Because the general characteristics seem to be more significant to an understanding of student teacher reflection than the individual differences within this group, the focus in this chapter is on the attributes themselves rather than on particular Alert Novices. Each of the features is described and analyzed through an examination of evidence from the Alert Novice cases and through a comparison and contrast of the relevant results from the case studies of both student groups.

PASSIONATE CREEDS

The Alert Novices appear to have been guided by a passionate creed. They had a certain mission to accomplish in their teaching. This strong belief seems to pervade the data associated with particular individuals, espe-

90

cially Heather, Laura, Denys, and Don. They mentioned it innumerable times in case investigation write-ups, case freewrites, pre-study and post-study questionnaires, and interviews. Their supervisors sometimes mentioned it also. The passionate creeds of each of these participants are described below, roughly in the order of the degree of intensity with which they appear to have been held.

Individual Passionate Creeds

Heather. Heather was a proponent of active learning and personal interpretation. She believed that the teacher should never impose a perspective on students; instead the teacher should help them to recognize and call upon their own resources and abilities in deriving information and drawing conclusions. The aim of the teacher is to develop student voices and imaginations. Quotations from several sources, including her pre-study questionnaire description of her best teacher, her post-study questionnaire response to "Why do you want to teach?", and a freewrite in her partner's lesson case, serve to illustrate:

> One of my high school English teachers . . . what was best about her was that she taught us how to think, not what to think. She gave us ways of thinking, perspectives, orientations. Then she asked us to use them, to adjust them to our minds and apply them. She encouraged intellectual exploration and creativity, she encouraged us to take risks and she supported us in our efforts, whether we succeeded or failed. She set an example for us to follow, but the example was not to be duplicated, it was to be interpreted. Learning is an act of interpretation, and as a teacher she performed the sister act to that—the act of revision.
>
> More specifically, I want to help my students develop the skills they will need to be aware of others, self-aware, and articulate about their awarenesses. Students need to learn to know their ideas, express them, and defend them. I want to help them believe that they have voices and that what they have to say is important. Students have their experiences and their imaginations to draw upon. What I can give them is the language and the confidence to use those things.
>
> I feel like they've picked up on my enthusiasm and feel comfortable. I thought as I was listening that they don't think twice about saying what they think—this says to me that they have acclimated to an environment in which their ideas are validated—and that's what I've tried to give them.

Heather's entire teacher case was devoted to this particular issue. She began it with a few lines of poetry about the power of the individual to overcome difficulties. The problem for this case investigation was the identification of the sources of her "philosophy of education," which she described in various instances as: "want[ing] them to have the idea that there isn't, at least most of the time, a right answer"; "the teacher should serve as guide, as moderator, as facilitator. By beginning with the experience of the students themselves, I am already beginning the process of empowering them"; "my main goal is to give the students the psychological and literal time and space to look inside themselves for direction and meaning."

The same passionate creed was described by Heather's supervisor in his summary evaluation of her: "Underlying thread to her teaching: students must learn to be active learners, must learn that they are responsible for making meaning and making decisions about rightness and wrongness of interpretations."

Laura. Laura was most concerned with her definition of *multicultural education.* Her passionate creed was to reduce the oppression of minority students and Third World peoples. She believed that the teacher must ensure equal opportunity for all students. In her pre-study questionnaire, Laura expressed interest in the university school of education because its focuses included "development, the Third World, literacy, and curriculum." Part of her response to the request for a definition of teaching was "facilitating the acquisition of skills needed to make decisions and act responsibly within society; fostering a student's sense of self-worth and dignity and the same in others."

In her post-study questionnaire[1] Laura answered the question "Why do you want to teach?" this way:

> The truth of the matter is that I want to teach because it is one of
> the few socially responsible occupations that I know of where you
> can also have a steady, livable income. I'm hoping that teaching will
> give me an opportunity to work in the Latino community. I also
> want to teach because it is active and appeals to a belief that people
> can learn and change.

Elsewhere in this document she was asked about the problems that were of most concern to her during the year. She responded:

> Probably the problem of most concern to me during the last school
> year was how to teach the subject matter to a very diverse group of

students, particularly to minority students who are essentially
tracked into lower level classes. I wanted the minority students to
come to my class and pass it (i.e., do their homework). I also had
hoped to help those students with reading in a social studies text-
book. On the subject matter side, I hoped too that my students
would come to appreciate distinctions between different peoples
and cultures and eliminate some of their ethnocentric, sometimes
xenophobic, attitudes.

All three of Laura's case investigations included, to varying degrees,
a consideration of this issue. The teacher case, entitled "Case Study: The
Possibilities of a Multicultural Class in a Multiethnic Classroom," was
directly devoted to the topic. In the freewrite accompanying the student
case, Laura took the opportunity to share her reactions to the general
structure of the Upward Bound program:

> It was a bit hard for me to sit in the back of the class for six weeks
> as one of the white authority figures observing minority students
> without being able to talk about that structure and the power rela-
> tions that maintain/derive from it. I'm not being clear: power in
> terms of student/teacher relationship; majority/minority relation-
> ship; rich/poor—the schism was dramatic. And we expect those
> kids to succeed by how we define success. Well, one might say, they
> would probably have the same definition . . . look at the rules they
> generate, they're our rules. But whose voice is speaking when a kid
> comes up with a rule that "two tardies and you're out of
> class"—does that de-mystify the power structure or further its rein-
> forcement? The internalization of oppression is powerful.
>
> Oh dear, I have gone off the deep end. Too much Paulo Freire.
> Well, it's fun to think about.

Denys. Denys was most anxious to promote spontaneity and creativity
in the classroom. He did not think it was important for the teacher to
provide structure or answers; instead the teacher should get students to
create and to think for themselves. An absence of dogmatism is critical.
His typically rather irreverent response to the pre-study questionnaire
question "Why do you want to teach?" is representative: "It provides a
dynamic atmosphere with *ideas* exchanged instead of a more static me-
dium. I feel a part of human *forward motion* as I open eyes and help in
guiding minds to a larger something intangible, and I'm good at it. Also,
July and August. Ties are not required. You needn't sell anything but the
truth however you see that." His post-study questionnaire response to the
same question: "Be a part of the evolution of mankind."

Denys's pre-study questionnaire description of his best teacher was also indicative of his passionate creed:

> Leonard was a wily old turkey who always kept us off balance. He could take any side of any issue and make you *want* to prove he was wrong. He'd get us so heated up over some issue which was just a blurb in the boring textbook, only to leave us knowing upon conclusion of the "discussion" that he really didn't know how he felt on the issue. He'd tell little anecdotes and cynically delineate some personality in his past analogous to some kid in the room and make everyone taste some of the absurdities we were living, only rarely offending those who could not recognize his brilliance. He *cared*, he was good.

The problems Denys identified for his teacher case were "How do I define worth and where do I get my recognition?" He never really came to any conclusions about these questions, admitting to their difficulty. He did, however, recognize that his definition of worth as a teacher "is predicated upon feelings," and that the feelings include enjoyment and a sense of mutual respect.

Denys's partner for the lesson case made several references to his "philosophy of teaching" in her write-up:

> Denys's style of teaching, as I have mentioned previously, does not subscribe to imposing structure on students' thoughts. He agrees with Norman that structure should be imparted, but Denys's perception of structure appears to be looser or less rigid than Norman's. In addition, he likes to play with knowledge in the classroom, making the atmosphere one of discovery (a "one never knows what may happen" kind of feeling). Denys conveys to the students the sense that he also is learning from their interaction. . . .
>
> Actually, much of Denys's teaching tries to reach the students on an attitudinal level; for example, he wanted them to reflect on whether they were "robots" and manipulated by the forces of culture. I must underline the fact that he does not intend to impart any particular attitude to the class, rather he hopes they will analyze their own position on topics he introduces.

Denys's supervisor made this comment in his summary evaluation: "Denys's greatest strength as a teacher is his creativity, his ability to see things in unique ways, and his desire to have his students see things in fresh ways. He uses varied techniques in teaching, and shows personal attention and sensitivity to his students."

Don. Don was particularly concerned with relevancy and consistency. He felt that the teacher must make the material relevant to students' lives and help in the development of their self-esteem. In addition, the teacher must be consistent in pedagogical techniques. When asked in an interview about his conception of good teaching, Don responded:

> It's very complex and I think consistency is important. . . . I think now I understand much better the importance of structure . . . good teaching makes material extremely relevant and interesting to kids and important to their daily lives and makes a real effort to tie things in, to make sense to them in order to have some value. I think it involves also a good understanding of their needs, which includes not necessarily educational needs, it does include that, but also their social needs and pressures.

Don's student case freewrite contained the following statement: "To me, these exchanges represent all the more reason for lessons and curriculum in schools to be relevant to the student's life." The final paragraph of his teacher case freewrite referred to his concern with the other key issue—consistency: "Also, another concern I have is that I feel as though I am in a *Catch-22* situation. I obviously need to continue to re-assess the situation and make changes in my class, but I feel that each change I make is invalidating a past change, and thus weakening the students' trust, confidence and judgment of me." The whole case investigation, in fact, devoted considerable attention to the subject of consistency. As he explored the control problems he was experiencing in his Spanish class, he cited the absence of routine as one of the probable sources of his difficulties. In the conclusion he stated: "I must minimize inconsistencies while continuing to experiment with various alternatives."

Kim. Kim believed in effective, honest communication between teachers and students. Her passionate creed was that teachers should help students to be creative problem solvers and should encourage them to care for one another and for their environment. When asked in the pre-study questionnaire about her reasons for wanting to teach, Kim replied: "I want to teach because I believe that we live in an increasingly complex world that requires creative and analytical problem solving." Her post-study questionnaire response to the same question was: "To help produce a more thoughtful generation of individuals who will creatively solve problems and care for Mother Earth."

Evidence of this belief also appears in her answers to the pre-study questionnaire questions about the definitions of teaching and learning:

Teaching is the ability to facilitate others to develop an interest to learn about something and continue to pursue that independently. Teaching is the ability to motivate others and to transfer valuable life-skills including critical thinking, creative problem solving and communication skills. Teaching is the ability to inspire others to continue to ask questions and investigate solutions.

Learning is the ability to acquire input (information, etc.) and process it so as to reach one's own conclusions about things. It is the ability to have analytical, communication, and creative-thinking skills and apply them to given situations.

Kim's teacher case was entitled "Stalking the Elusive Honest Moment (A Neophyte Reflects)." The problem for this study was to clarify her philosophy of teaching: "The task before me has been to arrive at a fuller understanding of what I mean by an 'honest bond' with my students or an 'honest moment' in the classroom. What is the depth and scope of this emerging philosophy? How does one begin and continue to foster these vital moments in the classroom?" She concluded her investigation as follows:

> Though I have really only begun to focus in on this intangible concept that I call honesty, the positive results of my attempts to reach students on an honest level encourage me to continue in this direction. My goal is to avoid the pitfall of the traditional adversarial teacher/student relationship and to learn to identify the opportunities in which to perpetuate honest moments. My hope is that I will relate with my students first, as another human being and second, as a teacher.

Gwen. Gwen also had an issue of central concern, although not quite as apparent as the passionate creeds of the other Alert Novices. She wanted students to think creatively and be independent from the impositions of society. Her pre-study questionnaire definition of learning was suggestive of this perspective: "Learning primarily involves the act of questioning and the formation of personal ideas. When one learns well, one attains the ability to analyze texts, theories, etc. in order to formulate a personal understanding of them. A good learner takes in specific information, but puts out a unique analysis and appreciation of that information." Her post-study questionnaire definition of teaching was also representative: "I think teaching involves encouraging students to critically think about the world, about themselves, about society . . . etc. That's why I enjoy teaching literature. It's a great way to examine values and practices that influence the kids' lives."

Both her pre- and post-study questionnaire responses to the question "Why do you want to teach?" referred to this principle:

> My desire to teach stems from both personal and general objective concerns. I have always had a great respect for education—for its ability to enable an individual to think creatively and to powerfully express those ideas. I want to try to convey this faith in education to students by trying to make it enjoyable and rewarding to learn. . . .
>
> My initial response to this question is that I want to teach students to think for themselves. I hope to get kids to question info they are fed by society and to reform their own values (which will hopefully be more egalitarian and reflective than many social norms).

Gwen's supervisor included this statement in her summary evaluation: "Gwen is a highly motivated, sensitive, and politically conscious young teacher."

All the Alert Novices had, to a greater or lesser extent, a passionate creed. A distinctive issue appeared several times in the data for each of these individuals. The same cannot be said for the majority of the Commonsense Thinkers. For four of them, Geoff, Andrea, Beth, and Rachel, no singular educational perspective could be detected in the data. Classroom management and organization was a pervasive concern, but I do not consider this to be of the same genre. A passionate creed has more to do with what a teacher wants to accomplish within a well-managed classroom. Although the creeds carry implications for management, they are not confined to that topic.

Now it may be that the Commonsense Thinkers did hold educational images that were simply not shared. I would suggest, however, that even if present, these beliefs are not likely to have been passionate creeds. A passionate creed, as I have defined it, is a belief held with intensity that permeates the teacher's thoughts about his or her teaching. If no evidence of such a belief appears anywhere in the data, it seems unlikely that it exists with intensity in the mind of the preservice teacher.

Two of the Commonsense Thinkers did seem to have an issue about which they were concerned; Carole and Paula did indeed appear to have passionate creeds.

Carole. Carole, an English teacher, worried about English as a Second Language (ESL) students and, in fact, did one of her field placements in an ESL classroom. An explicit mention of the ESL issue occurred three times in the data, two in responses on her post-study questionnaire:

> I have really had to deal with the issue of multiability students in a single classroom. In ESL some students spoke little English and were sharp, some spoke little English and were dull—teaching the two groups at once was difficult—took extra planning. Need to be sensitive to their needs—not just "special needs," but everyone.
>
> One problem was in the ESL class and I tried to use simple language and visual aids and oral reading so basic ability students would understand topic of discussion or reading material. The brighter students would take the discussion further and I had a hard time drawing the lower ability back in. I would ask them simple questions after repeating/condensing the discussion interaction. Usually that worked. If I had a hard time teaching vocabulary—visual aids, objects or drawings worked well. Useful in mainstream classes with ESL kids as well.

The one other instance, which is more on the philosophical level, appeared in her student case freewrite:

> Studying her and her brother also brought out my concern for the treatment of minorities in education, especially those ESL students who must face a new language and a new culture while they are attempting to learn. Many of the teachers, even in the program, disturbed me by the way they handled ESL kids in their classrooms—my question (and one I will work on in the future) is why can't we emphasize speaking as well as writing across the curriculum? I can see that I will lose patience with teachers who do not "try" to draw their foreign students out into the classroom.

Paula. Paula's passionate creed had to do with the development of positive personal and interpersonal values, particularly as they relate to minority and bilingual students. Her pre-study and post-study questionnaire responses were indicative of this:

> There are many reasons for my wanting to teach, including: getting involved with young people's development and thinking; being a positive role model; caring and working toward students' positive self-esteem; wanting to convey a sense of responsibility and commitment to oneself and to mankind. . . .
>
> Teaching is a real opportunity to work with young and usually

energetic people who may not have clearly developed their view of the world or its people. Since I have a strong commitment to certain values, I feel that teaching allows me to foster these values in my students (i.e., cooperation, individual and international, safety, respect, commitment, etc.). I am also personally concerned about students who may need someone to treat them as if they "matter."

In her student case freewrite Paula talked about the value of getting to know her students well and also about how difficult it would be to do so. She also shared at length her concerns about providing guidance for and instilling motivation in minority students in the Upward Bound program. Paula was a psychology and a social studies teacher.

General Aspects of Passionate Creeds

One aspect of these passionate creeds worth noting is the tendency for the beliefs to be associated with the disciplinary backgrounds of the Alert Novices who held them. Heather and Gwen, for instance, were both English teachers; their passionate creeds related to the idea of personal interpretation. They wanted their students to be able to think for themselves and to value their own voices and imaginations. Laura and Denys were social studies teachers. Their views were similar to those of the English teachers in that they favored independent thinking. Laura in particular couched her values in more political terms; she was most concerned about reducing the oppression of minority students and Third World peoples. Denys spoke about the absence of dogmatism, but Gwen also mentioned a need for students to think independently of the impositions of society. Kim, who was both an English and a social studies teacher, referred to creativity in terms of problem solving. She favored open communication between teacher and student and emphasized a need for students to learn to care for their environment. Her background included years of experience as an outdoor educator and wilderness tour guide. Don was a psychology and Spanish teacher whose undergraduate major was psychology, with an emphasis in adolescent development. He was most concerned with making material relevant to students' lives and with creating a consistent and comfortably predictable environment.

Also of interest in regard to subject-matter background is that none of the Alert Novices in the study were from the areas of science or mathematics, whereas three of the Commonsense Thinkers, Geoff, Andrea, and Beth, were. Perhaps this is an indication that reflection is different from logical thinking, as traditionally defined, since such logical thinking is typically associated most closely with the disciplines of mathematics and science. In a study by Morine-Dershimer (1987), for instance, "Science/ math majors . . . tended to display patterns of thought associated with logical reasoning more frequently than English/social studies majors" (p. 12). The details of these potential relationships were not a focus of this study and cannot be determined from the available data.

Another noteworthy aspect of the data on passionate creeds is that five of the six Alert Novices chose their passionate creed to be the topic for their teacher case. The assignment was open-ended, asking them to reflect upon any issue or aspect of their teaching that seemed particularly salient during the period of investigation. Given those circumstances, most of them chose to consider, either directly or indirectly, their passionate creed. The only exception was Gwen, the one whose belief seemed the least intensely held. She explored the differences between her instructional techniques in the two classes she was teaching and the reasons behind those differences.

Since most of the Commonsense Thinkers did not have a passionate creed, creeds were obviously not the topics for their teacher cases. What, then, were the foci for the Commonsense Thinker teacher cases? For Andrea, Geoff, and Beth the topic was classroom management. They were concerned about control problems they were experiencing. It should be noted that Don, an Alert Novice, also wrote about his difficulties with discipline, but included in his discussion was a consideration of the issue of consistency—one of his major concerns. The other three Commonsense Thinkers explored general pedagogical issues. Rachel, for instance, discussed techniques conducive to the learning process. Carole described the regimental features of the English curriculum at her high school. She was one of the two with a passionate creed, but her ESL issue was not included in this case. Paula's teacher case addressed two areas she thought required her constant attention: "(1) presentation of the course content with a multicultural perspective (via SPICE) and, (2) structuring the course information in a more organized form in order to facilitate student note-taking and understanding." The first topic was representative of Paula's passionate creed. Overall, when given the opportunity to investigate an issue of great concern to them, these Commonsense Thinkers chose to focus on general pedagogical techniques or matters of classroom control. These results suggest that assigning student teachers to reflect on an issue of interest may help reveal both whether they have passionate creeds and, if they do, what those creeds might be.

The specific nature of passionate creeds, their development and operation, requires further research and discussion. It may be that they are very similar to Dewey's (1932) moral principles. He proposes that:

> The object of moral principles is to supply standpoints and methods which will enable the individual to make for himself an analysis of the elements of good and evil in the particular situation in which he finds himself. . . . [It] gives the agent a basis for looking at and examining a particular question that comes up. . . . It economizes his thinking by supplying him with the main heads by reference to which to consider the bearings of his desires and purposes; it guides him in his thinking by suggesting to him the important considerations for which he should be on the lookout. (p. 141)

The Alert Novices did seem to use passionate creeds both as focal topics and as means by which to judge the other aspects of their teaching. Kim, for instance, devoted attention to what she meant by honesty in the classroom, and she judged her performance as a teacher on the basis of whether or not she was promoting honest communication between herself and her students. The passionate creed can be both the content of and the impetus for student teacher reflection.

The passion portion of this concept may be comparable to the emotion of excitement, as described by Izard (1977): "The emotion that plays the most crucial role in determining the complexity and quality of consciousness and life itself, is interest—excitement. For what you are, and what you are most conscious of, is what excites you" (p. 147). These creeds are what the Alert Novices were most conscious of in relation to their teaching. Their interest in these issues seemed to motivate them to both produce the appropriate conditions and reflect upon the associated meanings and the outcomes.

The concept of passionate creed may also be similar to Elbaz's (1983) concept of "images." In her scheme, images are the least explicit and most inclusive level of practical knowledge. They help to mediate among competing principles and rules. "On this level, the teacher's feelings, values, needs and beliefs combine as she forms images of how teaching should be, and marshals experience, theoretical knowledge, school folklore, to give substance to these images" (p. 134). She suggests that images are "something one responds *to* rather than acting *from*"; they "pull" rather than "push," inspire rather than require conformity. The passionate creeds of the Alert Novices did seem to inspire them to achieve a certain image of teaching. They were motivated by these images to create a particular environment; they were not just reacting to educational events. It is possible that reflection in teacher education may help novices both to modify their early images or passionate creeds as necessary and to translate them into appropriate practical principles and rules, the other levels of Elbaz's practical knowledge.

Passionate creeds may also be aspects of what Valli (1990) refers to as the relational and critical approaches to reflective practice. Teachers following a relational approach have student growth needs as a central concern. They attempt to create a caring community in part by inviting and listening to the voices of the cared-for. Such terminology is reminiscent of Heather's desire to develop her students' voices and validate their personal experiences and ideas; Don's wish for classroom experiences to be relevant to students' lives; and Kim's belief in effective, honest communication between students and teachers.

In Valli's (1990) analysis, teachers using a critical approach have "a preferential concern for the oppressed and disadvantaged" (p. 48) and see schools/classrooms "as sites for personal empowerment and social transformation" (p. 48). These notions were apparent in Laura's desire to reduce the oppression of minority students and Third World peoples, Denys's wish for an absence of dogmatism in the classroom, and Gwen's aim of having students think creatively and be independent from the impositions of society. The distinctions Valli makes are in reference to teacher education programs rather than to individual student teachers. Nonetheless, the presence of the distinguishing features of these two moral approaches to reflective teacher education, the relational and the critical, in the passionate creeds of the Alert Novices has some interesting implications. For example, the presence in these student teachers of the attitudes such programs attempt to develop lends credence to the identification of these individuals as having reflective propensities. Also, since two different approaches seem to be represented in this group, it may be that programs ought to use different approaches for different individuals, depending upon their passionate creeds, rather than the same program for all. Perhaps different individuals could preserve and expand upon their creeds within a general frame of moral deliberation.

Though the influence of these passionate creeds on the reflective process seems to be in the main positive, these beliefs can also serve as barriers to reflection. First, the belief may be held with such fervor that it is never subjected to the reflective process. Regardless of the "nobility" or "rightness" of the creed, such conviction is problematic in that it is counter to the attitudes of reflection and thus may limit the growth and development of the individual. In Dewey's (1932) words: "The 'good' man who rests on his oars; who permits himself to be propelled simply by the momentum of his attained right habits, loses alertness; he ceases to be on the lookout. With that loss, his goodness drops away from him" (p. 132).

The problem can be exacerbated by the fact that the passionate creed may not be the result of a reflective process. As Hullfish and Smith (1961) observe, a "readiness to act may be caused by processes which are uncontrolled by thoughtful grounding activity. Beliefs may be 'fixed' by a single emotional experience, or they may be ingrained by prolonged or intensive conditioning" (p. 52). Or they may be intuitions never subjected to deliberation and unsubstantiated by adequate evidence (Dewey, 1932). "Even when beliefs may be said to be *correct,* unless they are grounded by the individual holding them, the best that can be said, under these circumstances, is that the individual has been properly *trained*. We cannot say that he has been soundly *educated*" (Hullfish & Smith, 1961, pp. 53–54).

Heather's teacher case, rated as indeterminate, is an example of this pitfall. In it she examined the sources of her beliefs about active student learning and personal interpretation, but she never questioned the beliefs themselves. What she discovered is that the origin of her passionate creed was her own experience as a learner. This excerpt from the associated freewrite is explanatory:

> The exciting thing about this process is becoming conscious of what I have been doing unconsciously. My supervisor has forced me to articulate my philosophy and dig back and discover its roots. Although I observed my master teachers for almost a full semester, I had in mind the kinds of things I wanted to do before that, and I didn't change my mind as a result of the observations. I didn't ask myself why I wanted to do it the way I did, it just seemed the clear and obvious way. I designed my units and lessons so that I would be starting where the students were and thereby making the material accessible to them. When I was forced to examine my choices and actions, I realized that the real models I had had were my own teachers, not the teachers I observed. I was acting on what had worked for me, what had generated my interest in literature and education. I realized that it was partly those models, and my being in classes led by professors who encouraged participation, that allowed me to be as articulate as I was about the process in which I am now engaged. I had internalized a model of teaching based on my own model of learning. The fact that I had drawn so extensively upon my own experience in the world in order to understand literature made it obvious to me that other students need to do that too. That that is what they would do if left to their own devices, and not forced to accommodate a learning model which might be completely inappropriate for them. I think of bound feet or corsets—growth is hindered. And that is often the way education is—so constructed, so oppressive, that students do not have room to explore, to discover their feeling and voice, to grow. I was able to

see in retrospect where my methods and enthusiasm came from and I can see now why I have attempted to recreate that kind of positive learning environment for my own students.

Though these beliefs do seem "noble" and "right," there are still questions to be raised: "What reason does she have for believing that what worked for her in her college courses should work for her high school students?" or "Are there any individual students or certain educational conditions that may require a different approach?" Heather gave no indication that she will ever raise such questions or that she sees any need to do so; thus her alertness, at least as regards this issue, may have been lost.

A secondary result of such lost alertness can be an overapplication of the passionate creed. The student teacher may carry the belief to extremes, invoking it in inappropriate ways in inappropriate circumstances. Heather's supervisor indicated in his interview that this may be a problem for her:

> She feels very strongly about some things, very strong willed about some of the stuff that she believes in about teaching. And it's such a noble thing that she's trying to do that at times, she's taking it a bit too far. . . . She's into not rescuing kids, like letting them struggle to discover, which is wonderful, because she's sick of the sort of rote formula approach to teaching English, dynamite, I mean I'm with her on that. But there were just a couple things she wasn't spelling out because she's so into not providing a formula that, that there were some things that the kids really needed.

He proceeded to describe the debriefing session they had had about a lesson he thought called for more modeling on her part. She disagreed with him and they "fought" over the issue, but he felt that the process was "enjoyable" and "valuable" because she came to understand her beliefs better and because she started to see his point. However, in the teacher case, where Heather documented this conversation, she reasserted her position and denied the value of his suggestion.

Denys's supervisor made a similar observation about Denys's belief in unstructured spontaneity and creativity in both the summary evaluation and an interview:

> His greatest weakness however, lies in his over reliance on a "performing" approach to teaching—i.e., relying too much on his own personal charisma and energy in the classroom, to produce learning. While there are certainly elements of drama and showmanship in teaching, Denys pushes this point too far.

I think Denys is a creative teacher, I think he thinks originally, he looks at things in an original way, in a fresh way, in non-conservative, unusual ways to the usual perspective. He tries to generate a lot of personal energy and enthusiasm in class . . . he generates a certain excitement in class that sometimes in his case turns out to be counter-productive because he gets the kids too high, too hyper. He tries to work on instinct at times in class. . . . Denys's instinct, at this time, I think, has more of his own personal need at a particular moment rather than what the class really needs at a particular moment.

Another potential pitfall of the passionate creed is that it can distract the preservice teacher from a consideration of other important issues. Laura admitted to such a distraction in her student case freewrite, a case scored as unreflective: "Also I liked the topic I chose for this paper because it had less to do with a study on personalities and more to do with analyzing the structure of a classroom and how that determines a kid's success." She was not doing a case investigation of an individual student; she was exploring the signs of the oppression of minorities in the overall program. In this case Laura's burning desire to end oppression was not only distracting, but also distorting. She did gather relevant and interesting evidence to explain the "success" of her case study subject, the only Caucasian in the Upward Bound program. However, she used it to argue that the program was oppressive to the minority students, without gathering evidence on the treatment or performance of these other students. She did not allow for the possibility of both Caucasian students and students of color succeeding in the same program. Granted it is better to err on the side of challenging the equity of the social structure than not; still that questioning needs to be well grounded and open to contradictory evidence.

Whether the influence of a passionate creed on preservice teacher reflection is positive or negative may depend in part on if and how these beliefs are challenged by the program. Hullfish and Smith (1961) suggest that a feeling of incongruency is a spur to reflection; but if the feeling of incongruency is experienced as threatening, the process may be bypassed. The latter is most likely when there is deep emotional attachment to the belief system, as is the case for passionate creeds. Their suggestion is that the calling into question of basic structures of meaning must be done gradually and in a safe environment.

The teacher case seemed to function as such a "safe environment" for most of the Alert Novices, since five of them chose their passionate creed as the topic for reflection in this case investigation. Laura's teacher case was most striking in this regard. Her beliefs about the importance of eliminating the oppression of minority students had been directly challenged by her initial experiences in teaching a multiracial social studies class. She saw herself doing those things she so adamantly opposed in the Upward Bound classrooms in her student case, such as rewarding students for conformity to the value system of the dominant culture and not adapting text material or lecture vocabulary for the less able readers. As a result, she took a good hard look at the problem, its roots, and its implications (which she had not done in the student case):

> Rather than creating an environment where all kids could learn and succeed, I had recreated a situation which encouraged white students to succeed and minority students to fail. The focus of this analysis is how this situation occurred, what ways can I generate classroom activities that encourage minority student success, and whether a classroom can become truly integrated.

In the course of her investigation, she came to realize that it is not as straightforward an issue as she may have thought it was. She explored the issue in depth, gathering and using data to come to understand what was actually occurring and why. She consulted others and obtained feedback from her students; she used her journal and documented her failed efforts. Laura acknowledged changes in her thinking and new insights: "I never considered that a multicultural education is as much *how* a subject is taught as what is taught." She was tentative in her conclusions and indicated important weak points in her efforts. Yet she did not abandon her fundamental values and goals:

> I am now questioning whether a classroom can become truly integrated when the larger society remains segregated. Can a classroom be a tool for social change? The history of the public school and its role within society would suggest that this is not possible. What I do hope to achieve in my classroom is a way of legitimizing minority culture in the deepest sense—a different way of communicating and approaching work that often differs from the dominant culture—fostering a sense of mutual respect and self-respect.

All the episodes in this case were scored as reflective.

Russell and Munby (1991) have found that "when an initial theory-in-action encounters puzzles or surprises, backtalk stimulates reframing, suggesting new actions that imply a revised theory-in-action. . . . Seeking consistency between theory and practice and better theories to guide practice appears to be an important element in productive reframing"

(p. 184). Thus to engage in reflection teachers need to have powerful theories, such as passionate creeds, to stimulate reframing, and they also need to experience dilemmas that challenge those theories. Laura's passionate creed was challenged by her experiences, prompting her to reevaluate and restructure both her theory and her actions.

The passionate creeds of preservice teachers not only can serve as powerful internal prods to reflection; they can become the focus, as Hullfish and Smith (1961) propose they need to be:

> The student needs to learn to find his *security in the process of growing,* not, as many may assume, in particular patterns of belief. As the student progressively gains control of the process within which his reconstruction occurs, he may then develop a toughness that will enable him to face increasing challenges to his beliefs without risk of serious personality damage. He may then not only learn to weather situations that require comprehensive reconstructions but, in addition, sharpen his sensitivity to incongruency. His potential for self-education will thus be increased. (p. 61)

All the Alert Novices appeared to have a passionate creed. This belief seemed to serve as an impetus for reflection; if nothing else, these new teachers were always asking themselves whether or not their classrooms reflected their basic philosophy. When given a choice of topic on the teacher case, most of them chose their passionate creed—they wanted to know more about it and how they were doing in relation to it. The creed did, on occasion, interfere with the reflective process, helping to account for two out of the four unreflective case investigations produced by Alert Novices—Laura's student case and Heather's teacher case. But since the influence seems to have been mainly positive and since all the Alert Novices have them, perhaps the beliefs and attitudes represented in passionate creeds are an identifying characteristic of the Alert Novice. Of course, two of the Commonsense Thinkers, Carole and Paula, also had passionate creeds. However, both Carole and Paula were Commonsense Thinkers because they had inquiry skill problems. Therefore, even though they had the desire to reflect and the internal impetus for doing so, they had trouble doing it. Alert Novices may need to have both the ability to reflect and the beliefs, values, attitudes, and emotions conducive to the process, the latter of which may be embodied in a passionate creed.

"WHY" QUESTIONS

Another feature that seems to have characterized the Alert Novices is the nature of the questions they asked. These teachers tended to see the process of reflection as asking "Why?": "Why am I teaching what I am teaching in the way that I am teaching it?" The question is directed at the roots of problems and the meanings of ideas and actions. Greene (1978) suggests that the "why" question may accompany and indeed "be necessary for an individual's moral life" because it is indicative of care, concern, and what she deems "wide-awakeness"; it helps individuals "to identify situations as moral ones or to set themselves to assessing their demands" (p. 43). In support of this argument, she quotes Camus: "One day the 'why' arises and everything begins in that weariness tinged with amazement" (cited in Greene, 1978, p. 43).

Individual "Why" Questions

Two of the Alert Novices explicitly included the "why" question in their written definitions of reflection—Kim in her post-study questionnaire and Gwen in her teacher case freewrite:

> To me, it means stepping back and looking at myself as a teacher and what/why/how I'm doing things in the classroom.

> I agree that it's important to teach us to reflect on our own teaching—after all that's what the program is all about. In compiling the data for this study we had to stop and consider what we'd been doing in the classroom and why we'd been doing it.

Denys was asked in an interview what it meant to him to be a reflective teacher: "Premise checking. You're going in there every day and doing something; why are you doing it? That's it. I think you tend to emphasize that a lot, step back and look at it, why are you doing it?" When probed further, he explained why "premise checking" was important to him:

> Well, if you're not looking at "why," you're going by some sort of training, by some sort of rote, it means that you're just perhaps following a path of least resistance and not really analyzing what is important; it's just like going down the road with blinders on. I mean you can make it from here to the other side but it isn't going to be a quality journey. . . . If I ever think that I know what I'm doing is right, I really want to step back and check my premise.

Denys used his teacher case to explore what he meant by a "quality journey" in the teaching profession. He struggled with how, in actual practice, he would be able to "check my premises." Denys made progress in isolating a few criteria and some means for obtaining feedback on his achievements in relation to those criteria. His conclusion provides evidence that he was not yet satisfied with his deductions in relation to an issue that he perceived as very crucial to his role:

> Perhaps as I grow as a human being and as a Teacher I'll be able to collate this feedback and incorporate it into my definition of worth and I'll be satisfied with my performance according to how I adhere to the tenets of this definition. Perhaps. Yet, I may never know what quality is as it pertains to educating a human being and the day I think I know I'll be scared to death. Certainly, even now I have criteria however vague upon which I base my feelings, yet I cannot escape from my question of, "is what I'm doing really endowed with quality?" and, "How have I defined quality?" As a person, I have notions of what quality is and try to conform to these, yet if I fail it is only myself that I have violated. As an educator however, my definition of quality will affect thousands of people and the question is a haunting one.

Kim also used the teacher case to explore the meaning of her philosophical beliefs. Several critical incidents in her classroom forced her to realize that she could not achieve her goal of honest communication unless she understood what she meant by it. Although she was able to formulate a definition, she admitted that the issue was complex. She concluded by recognizing that she had to continue to grapple with the roots and ramifications of her values.

Don did not mention the "why" question directly but hinted at it several times in his interviews. For example, when asked for suggestions about how to make the case assignment more conducive to reflection, he responded:

> Anything that would require more of a broad outlook on our teaching experience. Or even that would require us to write our overall philosophical views on something, just so we know what those philosophical views are. You know, just as we try to get the students to clarify their values and to understand it, be judgmental and all those things, we need to do that for ourselves as well.

The "why" question framed the problem in Heather's teacher case: She wanted to know why she believed in active learning. In her associated freewrite, however, she gave the impression that she saw the asking of this question as a "one-time" experience. She asked "why" in this case investigation in order to determine the source of her beliefs, and she was surprised by what she learned. But now that she "knew" the answer, she did not have to ask it again. If she did, she could always say, "I am doing what I am doing because students should be active learners." This pitfall of the passionate creed was discussed in the previous section.

Laura did not overtly refer to the "why" question. However, her lesson case was an exploration and acknowledgment of the role of perspective and conceptual framework in teaching and the interpretation of teaching. For this assignment Laura had observed a fellow social studies teacher teaching a European history lesson on the Revolutions of 1848. In the course of doing the project, Laura discovered that she and her partner had very different interpretations of the content and outcome of the lesson. The resulting case investigation write-up portrays a fascinating deliberation and struggle with an instance of schema clash between Laura and the teacher, concluding as follows:

> One of the principle problems that I have encountered in my analysis of Tammy's lesson was how my own "lens" affected my understanding of what went on in the classroom and within the heads of her students. Tammy's conception of political history was largely formulated through her study of American history; mine was developed through the study of Latin American history. Her analysis comes out of the tradition of English and European liberalism; mine comes from a Marxist analysis. Her usage of many of the terms in her lesson was consistent with her theoretical understanding. I have a different conception for many of those terms because of my theoretical background. For example, I would never employ a heuristic device of a political spectrum to elucidate political movements since I understand them to be the result of class conflict. My "structure" or interpretation of history reflects my own analysis. What were misconceptions in my mind as to the students' understanding of the Revolutions of 1848 may have been perfectly consistent with the interpretation of history that Tammy is presenting in her classroom.

The two freewrites accompanying this case investigation continued the deliberation, as an excerpt from one exemplifies:

> I think, though, that she did achieve her goals in terms of knowledge level understanding and providing a framework for the kids to hang that info. I just question the framework as actually reflective of that deeper structure. But if history is interpretation, then she has one way of interpreting it and I have another. I think that the

differences lay in different political philosophies more than in a mis-
use of Schwab's syntax. Maybe it's a question of what he refers to
as substantive structure. My conception of political history was formulated through studying Latin America, Tammy's through her
study of the U. S. How can those two experiences be applied when
looking at European political history?

Laura overrode her initial impression that the content and organization of Tammy's lesson was simply wrong and engaged in an effort to
understand why Tammy taught the Revolutions of 1848 the way she did.
In doing so, she recognized and confirmed the role of the teacher's philosophical perspective in the teaching process.

General Aspects of "Why" Questions

The Alert Novices were concerned with why they were doing what they
were doing and with the meanings and implications of their values and
philosophies or passionate creeds. In contrast, only two of the Commonsense Thinkers mentioned the "why" question. Rachel did so in one of
the freewrites for her partner's lesson case, the case where her own lesson
had been under investigation:

> Talking with Sandra after the lesson (and pre-lesson) really made
> me seriously consider my objectives and reasons for teaching the les-
> son—it also helped in organizing where the emphases for my lesson
> would be. Sandra's barrage of questions made me think and rethink
> why I was doing what I wanted to do and how I might implement
> some of the ideas that came up.

Rachel gave little other indication of her attitude toward reflection in general or the asking of "why" in particular. She did try to explore what
she meant by the "process of learning" in her teacher case. However, as
previously described, a confusion of terms minimized and distorted the
productivity of this effort. She also mentioned twice that she should continue to gather evidence and to think about issues, but her freewrites
were, in the main, a further discussion of the topic of the case investigation rather than a reaction to the experience. She did not answer the post-
study questionnaire question on the definition of reflection.

Paula asked the "why" question in her third interview. She had been
discussing her efforts to help students keep good notes in special notebooks, which she had been told by many parties was important to do.
She had come up with one idea for obtaining student response, but only

four students had done so. She was, however, pleased with the quality of these notes. Following this account, she commented: "Afterward you think about 'Why do I want a notebook and is it really just to make sure that they're paying attention?' And I don't think that's the reason. So I have to figure it out." She began to do so in the interview, but veered off onto another topic.

Paula had a positive attitude toward reflection and toward the program requirements along those lines. Her post-study questionnaire answer to the question about reflection is representative: "I think I am a 'reflective' person. I have always been concerned about what I choose to do, how I do it, considering the implications of what I do, how I might make it better, etc. The program helped sharpen this innate trait of mine —in terms of helping me focus on particular issues and concerns related to teaching." Paula wanted to reflect and, in fact, saw herself as doing so. She just did not seem to be able to carry out the process fully.

No evidence of the "why" question appeared in any of the data for the other four Commonsense Thinkers. Again, of course, such an absence does not mean that they never ask the question; one can only say that it is not present in the data. What is present, however, is a different kind of question: These individuals tended to ask "how" questions—"How do I plan an organized lecture?" or "How do I get my classroom under control?" They were concerned with "what works."

The topics they chose for the teacher cases—classroom management and organization—were indicative of this orientation. Andrea, Geoff, and Beth explored issues of classroom control. In a sense they did ask a "why" question—"Why is my classroom out of control?" They asked the question, however, in order to discover *what* to do to regain control. They were not asking why they were teaching what they were teaching in the ways they were teaching it; they were not asking about the meaning or implications of their beliefs or actions. Carole described her high school's regimented English curriculum and disciplinary program and shared some of her efforts to cope with the circumstances. The account remained at the surface level, however; she did not explore the reasons behind either the system's structure or her reactions.

Paula's teacher case was similarly descriptive. She chronicled her efforts to present the course content in a multicultural perspective and to structure the course information in a more organized way. In the process of listing these events, she did exhibit some tentativeness in her deductions, did use and even question the input of her observers, did consider evidence counter to her first reactions (but not counter to her initial proposals), and did show some change of views. However, she did not examine or question her own beliefs and often evaluated her success in achieving those taken-for-granted goals simply on the basis of "what works." For example, she cited the following as support for her conclusion that her "attempts to present an 'organized multicultural perspective' on personality development and abnormal behavior did succeed to some degree":

> Additionally, my Master Teacher observed my class during the third week of this project. He commented that the material was presented clearly and that I had made connections between different ideas which had been presented during this lesson and/or in previous lessons. "At least I know that sometimes I am doing it right." (straight from my journal!)

Paula did not discuss this notation. She raised no questions about the judgment of her master teacher; for example, she did not observe that neither of them had either considered or determined what the students learned from the lesson.

Beth's teacher case was replete with examples of "what works" judgments. Like Paula, she used the case investigation to chronicle her efforts in relation to her topic—classroom control. But her discussion of each attempt contained even less evidence of reflectivity; she made no reference to input from her observers, and she analyzed neither the potential reasons behind the success or failure of the techniques nor their implications. As an example:

> WEEK 3—This is the week to start worrying about the classroom management issue. Appropriately, the student who had been suspended from class returned. I had learned about troubles he had been having at home. I felt very sorry for him and I wanted to help him in any way I could. He seemed to be eager to come back to class. I wrote a contract for him to sign and follow, if I were to give him a second chance to be in the class. He was to refrain from disruptive behavior and catch up with the class by doing extra assignments. He was supposed to have the contract signed by his parent. The very first day after being quiet for 20 minutes he started talking to neighbors and not paying attention to classwork. I cautioned him softly and encouraged him to answer questions so he would start getting his confidence back. He took a test that he had missed and scored very well. I was very optimistic about the student. The student did not get the contract signed by his parent even by Friday and lied about it. I was very disappointed. I had gone out on a limb for him because I believed that he was a bright student and a sense

of achievement would help him put his personal problems behind him.

This was Beth's entire discussion of the incident. The implication is that it represented an example of failure in her efforts to control the class, but that, in this instance at least, the fault lay with the student. She did not explore the myriad of issues embedded within the situation, the most obvious of which was the parent signature requirement for a student with "troubles at home."

The topic for Geoff's teacher case was also classroom management; he was concerned with discovering why his geometry class had become bored so that he could figure out what to do about it. This case investigation was scored as reflective because he did engage in a thorough effort to determine the source of the problem and to pursue a number of alternative solutions. He used input from a variety of sources, including the research and theory presented in the teacher education program, and most of his judgments were appropriately tempered. However, the ultimate basis for these judgments was "what works," as can be seen in this unreflective episode:

> Another time I put together a simple worksheet that I thought might help in learning proofs. I've never seen a group of kids work so hard in my life! The response was tremendous and I've had requests for additional such worksheets. Sometimes getting a clear idea of what you hope to accomplish in a class period is 75% of the problem.

Geoff's performance on this case investigation reveals an interesting feature of his "what works" criterion: Geoff was encouraged to reflect and did reflect when his efforts to resolve a problem did *not* work, but he did not engage in reflection when they did work. "Just why things were going so great I never bothered to inquire." He saw the purpose of evaluation as the identification of "what went wrong." In Hullfish and Smith's (1961) words, "the *feeling* of incongruency acts as a spur" (p. 54) to reflection. Geoff's conclusions about the "successful" worksheet, however, seem also to call for in-depth analysis and evaluation. Things that "are working" are in need of as much reflective consideration as things that are not. If nothing else, teachers should consider what they mean by success and how they can tell whether they have achieved it. As Shulman (1986b) observes: "The teacher need not only understand *that* something is so; the teacher must further understand *why* it is so, on what grounds its warrant can be asserted, and under what circumstances our belief in its justification can be weakened or even denied" (p. 9). Shulman is here referring to subject-matter content, but the same seems to be true of knowledge about pedagogy.

Reflective teachers reflect about what works as well as about what does not. The Alert Novices may have been more likely to do so because they seemed to be driven by the question of "why." They asked why they were teaching what they were teaching in the way they were teaching it, regardless of whether or not they felt successful. The Commonsense Thinkers, on the other hand, tended to ask "What works?" This question not only limits the occasions for reflection to instances of perceived failure; it also serves to keep any analysis at a surface level. Beliefs and practices only need be evaluated in relation to one criterion: "Is it working?" Furthermore, classroom strategies and acts, apart from their meanings and implications, are the sole focus of attention in this question. Underlying belief and value systems are overlooked, making the content of reflection very narrow.

As in Gore and Zeichner's (1991) student projects, "the lack of 'critical reflection' in many of the reports is not so much a question of the topic as it is a question of the way the topic is framed" (p. 132). The questions student teachers ask frame the topics they investigate; it makes a difference whether they ask "why?" or "what works?" As Ross (1987) suggests, reflective teacher education programs need to help students move beyond a consideration of "what works." Similarly, Adler (1991) advocates assisting student teachers in developing "the ability to make decisions about teaching and learning which demonstrate awareness of ethical and political consequences and of the possibilities of alternatives" (p. 78). One way to do this, according to him and to Tabachnick and Zeichner (1991), is to continue to ask novices why they did what they did; then they can "become interested in probing the purposes of their work and in thinking about its consequences" (Tabachnick & Zeichner, 1991, p. 15). According to Greene (1978), such an effort cannot be overlooked, because the asking of "why" initiates learning and moral reasoning. The Alert Novices in this study seem already to have been asking that question for themselves.

CONCLUSION

We see examples of both beginning and experienced teachers who are willing to articulate their puzzles and their reflections as they attempt to make sense of theoretical perspectives on teaching in terms of their own practical experiences. We also see beginning and experienced teachers who seem unable to reflect on their practices, unable to reframe their problems, and unable to interpret their practices in more than one way. (Russell et al., 1988, p. 88)

Among the participants in this study, I also see examples of both. The case studies contribute to the development of our understanding of those differences (see Table 5.1 for a summary of the case study results). First, some of the Commonsense Thinkers had problems with cognitive processing. These individuals may simply not have had the skills to carry out sophisticated reflective tasks, such as the lesson case investigation. Others had beliefs, values, attitudes, or emotions that interfered with the reflective process. Though capable, these student teachers were unlikely

TABLE 5.1 Summary of case study results

		"Passionate Creed"	"Why" Questions	Reason for Categorization as Commonsense Thinker
Common-sense Thinkers	Carole	Yes	No	Inability
	Geoff	No	No	Emotions
	Rachel	No	Yes	Emotions
	Paula	Yes	Yes	Inability
	Andrea	No	No	Emotions
	Beth	No	No	Inability
Alert Novices	Gwen	Yes	Yes	
	Denys	Yes	Yes	
	Kim	Yes	Yes	
	Heather	Yes	Yes	
	Don	Yes	Yes	
	Laura	Yes	No	

to reflect, particularly in spontaneous situations. They required strong incentives and facilitative structures that varied by individual. The four reflective case investigations produced by the Commonsense Thinkers include an example from each case assignment.

Thus both inquiry skills and conducive beliefs, values, attitudes, and
emotions seemed to characterize the Alert Novices. They were not only
capable of reflective thought processes; they seemed also to have an internal impetus for doing so. They were pushed to be reflective about their
teaching, even when they preferred not to, as is demonstrated in these
quotations from Kim's and Gwen's teacher case freewrites:

> I found this self-evaluation extremely useful. On the other hand, I
> was, at times, frustrated by the prospect of having to take critical
> time out from my lesson planning/paper grading cycle to ponder
> greater questions. There is always the possibility that too much re-
> flection too soon will hinder our teaching at this point. There are
> too many things that one can get caught up in not the least of
> which is some of the tragic lives led by our students. Then one be-
> gins to wonder what one's role is in teaching. Whether it's possible
> to make small changes in our students' lives or whether we're per-
> haps in the wrong profession. Sometimes early on, one has to
> mostly *do* and think about it later.

> I think that this assignment is excellent in theory, yet I question its
> effectiveness in practice. I agree that it's important to teach us to re-
> flect on our own teaching—after all that's what the program is all
> about. In compiling the data for this study we had to stop and con-
> sider what we'd been doing in the classroom and why we'd been do-
> ing it. Great . . . we need to have this practice instilled in us, and I
> believe that the case study was successful in accomplishing this
> goal. However, considering how overwhelmed all the students are
> at this stage in our teaching career, I don't think that we were able
> to get nearly as much out of this as one may have hoped. . . . I of-
> ten felt that this assignment was more of a burden than an en-
> riching exercise.

Part of this internal impetus seems to derive from a passionate creed.
The Alert Novices had strong beliefs that guided their thoughts and decisions in relation to teaching. They were very concerned about whether or
not their teaching was consistent with their passionate creeds. Most of
the Commonsense Thinkers did not have such a passionate creed. The
two who did, Carole and Paula, appear to have had problems with the

processes of reflective thinking. Thus they may have had an impetus to reflect but were not capable of doing so.

Another part of the impetus may result from asking "why?" Alert Novices tended to ask why they were teaching what they were teaching in the way they were teaching it. In contrast, Commonsense Thinkers tended to ask "what works?" The asking of "why" questions is more compatible with the process of reflection as defined in this study. Such an orientation encourages the examination of meanings and sources of beliefs and problems and the critical scrutiny of classroom decisions and outcomes.

The conducive orientations of the Alert Novices not only served as an impetus for reflection but also influenced the process of reflection. In other words, these beliefs, values, attitudes, and emotions also helped to determine whether or not the consideration of an educational event or idea was an act of reflection at all. Alert Novices seemed to see the value of open-mindedness, responsibility, and whole-heartedness and reflect that in their deliberations. They tended to suspend judgment during investigation, to cast about for evidence and counterevidence from multiple sources about a variety of alternatives, and to temper their conclusions. The case studies are replete with such examples of both spontaneous and structured reflection. Particularly exemplary of the latter are Laura's and Gwen's teacher cases and Kim's lesson case. The following more concise examples from Don's pre-study questionnaire and Denys's student case freewrite also serve to illustrate this point[2]:

> "Describe what it will be like to be a teacher in a classroom."—
> Being a teacher will be an ongoing experience of reassessment and of questioning. How do I present material? Why? What benefit should students gain? Am I teaching something that will be relevant later? Can the skills be used, transferred to other situations? Etc. etc. etc.

> I learned a hell of a lot in this experience and view it as one of our most valuable activities in becoming teachers. I learned these people are playing with a vastly different deck of cards than I have been dealing with as a student. I've traveled about the world enriching myself with the disparate views of peoples from other cultures while 10 miles from where I grew up, a girl like my subject is living a life as rich in its difference as those I've experienced on the globe—both sides. My student speaks Spanish at home, has eleven brothers and sisters, is not allowed to go out unless accompanied by family, is encouraged to be with the family when she'd rather be reading, she gladly donates all of her hard earned money to the fam-

ily coffers and is discouraged in many pursuits where I was encouraged. Wow! I've learned how much we project our feelings onto others, after all, that is the manner in which we process information,
but if I'm trying to understand what a limbless person feels like,
I'm merely viewing it as a limbless person with arms and legs
which *isn't* it. I'm trying to understand her life in my context and
it's not it either. I'm projecting how I would feel, but the fact is . . .
I don't know. I want to make a conclusion and define a problem,
and perhaps I can logically arrange my data so that a strong case is
made to prove a point, but it's just me imposing something on someone else. Research is damn difficult if one wants to emerge with a
clear picture. Fabulous time. These little faces have lives and their
little dramas are altogether as important as mine, and when these
intersect, and at only that one small point of intersection, we touch
and that's it, but it isn't.

Pro-Active vs. Reactive Orientations

Before closing this discussion, I will readdress the issue of misplacement.
I still acknowledge that the participants in this study may have been
placed in the wrong comparison group. It may be that some supposed
Commonsense Thinkers were just being flippant or contrary or lazy. It
could be that they engaged in thought processes they did not or could not
share verbally. Perhaps the Alert Novices were simply more eloquent.
There were, after all, four instances in which the Alert Novices did not
produce a reflective case and four instances in which the Commonsense
Thinkers did. Nonetheless, I believe that there is evidence in the data that
helps to explain these results in terms consistent with the conclusions being drawn: The reflective case investigations written by Commonsense
Thinkers were all produced by students who had the ability to reflect but
not the internal impetus to do so. They were able to reflect when the
conditions minimized their particular emotional or attitudinal interferences. The Alert Novices were not expected to be perfect in their reflective
propensities or efforts; thus instances of unreflective thinking were not
inconsistent with their categorization, especially if other factors seem to
explain their performance. In two of their unreflective case investigations—Laura's student case and Heather's teacher case—they either over-
extended or were distracted by their passionate creeds. In the other two
—Heather's and Kim's student cases—the particular topic or situation
seemed to trigger an emotional state that interfered with the reflective
process. Heather may have overidentified with her subject, and Kim may
have been overly resistant to any emotional attachment to her student.[3]

At any rate, real differences in the reflective thought processes and orientations of the two groups do seem to emerge from the data. Geoff, a Commonsense Thinker, and Heather, an Alert Novice, both produced a reflective, an unreflective, and an indeterminate case. A problem for both of them was their overconfidence about their abilities as teachers. Heather, however, had a passionate creed that provided her with an internal impetus for reflection, which Geoff did not seem to have. In addition, Heather was concerned with why she was teaching as she was, whereas Geoff evaluated his efforts more in terms of "what works." Her reflection was on a deeper level, concerned with the sources and meanings of beliefs and ideas. He was reflective only when he thought things were not working, while her reflective activity was more pervasive, including unstructured situations (such as the pre-study questionnaire) and "successful" situations (such as her efforts to engage students in active learning).

Laura, an Alert Novice, and Andrea, a Commonsense Thinker, both produced two reflective case investigations and an unreflective student case. But again, there were substantial differences between the two. Laura was driven by and reflective about a passionate creed. The main reason for her unreflective case investigation was that she devoted her attention to this issue when the topic for the case was meant to be otherwise and the data she had gathered was inappropriate. Laura was concerned about the meaning and implication of her conceptual framework for the design and interpretation of her teaching. Andrea produced no evidence of either a passionate creed or the asking of "why" questions. Her reflective ability seemed to be hampered by severe problems with self-esteem. She could reflect about this lack of self-esteem, as she did so well in her teacher case, and she could reflect about the teaching of others, as she did in the lesson case. However, she could not seem to reflect about any other personal educational issue. Her identification with her student case investigation subject and consequent dislike of his personality appeared to contribute significantly to the production of an unreflective student case. Of the 50 original participants, Andrea received the most unreflective total score on the pre-study questionnaire. Her emotional interference was more extensive and more consistent than the emotional interferences experienced by Kim and Heather in the production of their student cases.[4]

In sum, the combination of the passionate creed and the "why" question seemed to produce for the Alert Novices a proactive orientation to teaching and problem solving. These student teachers said to themselves, "I will go out and do this specific thing, because I believe such and so." The Commonsense Thinkers had more of a reactive orientation. They seemed to say, "I tried this and it didn't work, so I'll try this." They appeared to be negatively motivated by the desire to prevent management

problems, whereas the Alert Novices were positively motivated to produce a certain environment. This distinction is captured by the responses
of Heather in her post-study questionnaire and Rachel in her pre-study
and post-study questionnaire to the question, "Why do you want to
teach?"

> I want to teach because I love to see people learn. I love to be able
> to facilitate the acquisition of knowledge; I love to guide students
> in their exploration of themselves and the world. I believe that my
> enthusiasm about this process is contagious. I communicate to stu-
> dents my love of knowledge and learning, and they see by my
> model that it can be an exciting thing. More specifically, I want to
> help my students develop the skills they will need to be aware of
> others, self-aware, and articulate about their awarenesses. Students
> need to learn to know their ideas, express them, and defend them. I
> want to help them believe that they have voices and that what they
> have to say is important. Students have their experiences and their
> imaginations to draw upon. What I can give them is the language
> and the confidence to use those things.

> When I graduated, I sat down and went through all the possible em-
> ployment ideas and opportunities that came to mind. Afterwards I
> went through and sifted out the ones I chose for monetary reasons.
> Then I went through and tossed the ones that interested me only
> slightly. After going through a few similar steps, the only idea left
> was teaching.
>   I want to contribute something more to society than I feel I
> could in a private sector job.

Alert Novices were not only more able to engage in acts of reflection,
they were more likely to do so. Commonsense Thinkers lacked either the
inquiry skills or the attitudinal, emotional orientations of reflective thinking—or both. These results carry important implications for policies,
practices, and research regarding reflective teacher education.

6

How to Help Reflection Happen

The reflective teacher—How could you not be one? Once a reflective teacher, always a reflective teacher, they say. But they should say, if not a reflective teacher, then never a teacher. Period.

(Brenda[1]—teacher case freewrite)

I agree with Brenda that teachers need to be reflective; reflective thinking, as I have defined it, is a necessary, though not sufficient, component of the teaching process. I think so for a number of reasons. First, teaching is an extraordinarily complex enterprise occurring in a social situation where the likelihood is high that the needs of one individual will be in conflict with those of another individual or with those of the group as a whole. Furthermore, the nature of those needs and conflicts can shift dramatically from moment to moment, depending upon a large array of contextual features. Even more challenging is the fact that these changing needs and conflicts are neither easily detected nor definitively interpretable. As Clandinin and Connelly (1991) note, "deliberation and reflection are methods for charting a meaningful though uncertain course in social affairs" (p. 263).

Because teachers' awareness and understanding of their students and classroom events will always be limited, they must gather and consider information about educational situations from multiple sources. They must temper their judgments and remain open to alternative interpretations and strategies. Their decisions and ideas must be subjected to frequent and careful reconsideration in light of information from current theory and practice, from feedback from the particular context, and from speculation about the moral and ethical consequences of their results. The

122

last of these underlies my second reason for believing that teachers need to be reflective.

A main goal of education, in my view, is a more just and humane world for students in particular and society in general. Thus teachers need to accept responsibility for the future as well as the present. Certainly the teacher must act in the moment, but to ensure that those actions are moving in a direction he or she wants, they must be evaluated in terms of both short-term and long-term needs and effects. Personal decisions and indeed institutional structures must be scrutinized to see whether or not all students are benefiting. Only in this way can teachers increase the possibility for more "tactful teaching" (Van Manen, 1991) and more equitable schooling.

The charge of the teaching profession is precious—the minds and lives of our children. We cannot afford to have teachers who are unwilling or unable to analyze the sources, meanings, and implications of their beliefs about their students and the learning process; who do not attempt to examine the nature of problems and their underlying causes or to explore alternative solutions; or who are too hasty, too certain, or too general in their evaluation of outcomes. Teachers must be explicit about what they are doing and why they are doing it. They must be vigilant in detecting the effects of these endeavors on individual students and in attempting to adapt future efforts to accommodate the new, though tentative, information.

Current theories in the cognitive psychology of learning are consistent with this perspective (Brown, Collins, & Duguid, 1989; Palincsar & Brown, 1984; Schoenfeld, 1985). Though there are variations and disagreements among these scholars, they are generally supportive of reflective attitudes and practices in teaching for the reasons cited above and for another that is suggestive of my third reason for why reflection is critical to good teaching. Student learning is dependent upon instructors who can model and make explicit an active engagement with subject matter, who can set problems as well as solve them. Teachers must be able to reflect publicly, in the presence of students, as well as privately. These theoretical notions add to the arguments in favor of reflectivity in teaching by proposing that it is not only consequential in teacher decision making and learning, it is also important to the encouragement of student learning and moral development.

The injunction for teacher educators, therefore, is to continue to struggle with ways to help novice teachers develop and/or nurture reflective attitudes and abilities. This study contributes to the literature on reflective teacher education by revealing issues, factors, and procedures that may prove useful in the endeavor. The study also poses implications for the recruitment and admission of preservice teachers and the assessment and support of inservice teachers.

REFLECTIVE TEACHER EDUCATION

A reflective teacher education program must know what it is trying to accomplish in order to accomplish it. The goals must be specific enough to serve as guides for the selection, design, implementation, and evaluation of structural aids to reflection and flexible enough to allow for adaptation to individual differences. The details matter, especially for Commonsense Thinkers who have difficulty with the procedures of reflection. Paula, for instance, seemed to benefit when the specifics of problem identification were spelled out in the assignment. Furthermore, the program's definition of reflection must be made explicit to all involved, including the student teachers. Otherwise, individuals will rely upon personal definitions of the term, as was apparent in the post-study questionnaire responses to this question: "This program aims to train reflective teachers. Do you think it does? If so, how? What does it mean to you to be a reflective teacher?" The definitions given by interns from both research groups varied. Kim offered this explanation: "It leaves a lot of it up to us to define what reflection means—the program doesn't tell us." Since beliefs about reflection have been shown to influence how student teachers engage in the process (Kitchener, 1983, 1986; Richert, 1987), efforts to improve the match with program conceptualizations are important. As Calderhead (1988) observes:

> Attempts to encourage student teachers to adopt an analytical, reflective and critical approach to the development of their own practice have sometimes been found to be resisted by those who hold alternative views of the process of learning to teach, such as modeling other teachers, or of following one's own instinct. (p. 76)

This study illustrates that if we are really serious about "changing 'reflective teaching' from a general, widely used slogan to a practical working principle" (Calderhead, 1989, p. 49), we must follow our own advice. Teacher education programs must be explicit about their aims and the meaning of those aims. Those of us in teacher education must continue to ask ourselves the questions Shulman (1988) poses to teachers: "How do I know what I know? How do I know the reasons for what I do? Why do I ask my students to perform or think in particular ways?" (p. 33). We cannot rely on intuition alone in the design and implementation of reflective strategies; our techniques may not be accomplishing what we think they are, especially if we are not clear about what it is we want to accomplish in the first place.

If the program definition eventually delineated and publicized is similar to the one I propose and advocate, then particular attention also needs to be given to the procedures and attitudes of reflection. Student teachers must be told what the procedures are, given instruction and assistance in how to carry them out, and provided with well-supported opportunities to practice what they have learned. Commonsense Thinkers who have inquiry skill problems may need particular help in this area. Both groups seem to need more instruction in the drawing of conclusions than in the setting of problems.

Even more importantly, a case needs to be made for suspended judgment, tentative conclusions, exploration of assumptions, active searching for evidence and counterevidence, consideration of ethical, social, and moral implications, and so forth. In this regard, special attention may need to be given to Commonsense Thinkers with interfering attitudes and values. The case investigation assignments used in this study did not emphasize the attitudes of reflective thinking as much as the procedures, and yet the presence or absence of these attitudes was the most critical factor in differentiating the reflective from the unreflective case investigations. Reflective teacher education programs should stress, therefore, the development of the "tact of teaching," an ethic of care and compassion, and a critical perspective on schooling; they can do this by encouraging the asking of "why" questions and capitalizing on and encouraging passionate creeds in individually appropriate ways.

The Asking of "Why?"

Greene (1978) argues that the "why" might be necessary for the living of a moral life, a state particularly important for teachers because one of their primary missions is to "combat mystification":

> I am convinced that, if teachers today are to initiate young people into an ethical existence, they themselves must attend more fully than they normally have to their own lives and its requirements; they have to break with the mechanical life, to overcome their own submergence in the habitual, even in what they conceive to be the virtuous, and ask the "why" with which learning and moral reasoning begin. (p. 46)

The results of this research tend to justify that perspective. The Alert Novices, the more reflective interns in this study, had a tendency to ask "why" questions—questions directed at the roots of problems and at the meanings of ideas and actions. They were concerned about the impact of their efforts on their students and were guided by such goals as the legitimation of student voice, the relevance of course materials, and the reduced oppression of students of color. The study does not tell us how the Alert Novices developed such propensities, however. These student teachers seemed to be inclined to ask "why" questions when they entered the program.

But the results are suggestive of efforts that might be made in reflective teacher education programs to help Commonsense Thinkers develop such inclinations. Most importantly, the finding that "why" questions did not tend to appear in any of the data for the Commonsense Thinkers, and thus were no more a part of their thinking later in the program than earlier, seems to corroborate a position held by Zeichner and Tabachnick (1991) and others (Britzman, 1986; Gore & Zeichner, 1991; Smyth, 1992) that simply trying to make student teachers more deliberative and intentional is not enough.

> Indeed, only when teachers take an active reflective stance, are they able to challenge the dominant factory metaphor of the way schools are conceived, organized and enacted. Being reflective, therefore, means more than merely being speculative; it means starting with reality, with seeing injustices, and beginning to overcome reality by reasserting the importance of learning. (Smyth, 1992, p. 300)

The case investigations and those of us who assigned, monitored, and evaluated them did not devote enough explicit attention to an interrogation of the status quo. We did not require, nor did we even suggest, that the student teachers ought to critique their institutional contexts. Greene (1978) and Van Manen (1991) maintain that if teachers are able to consider alternative points of view, particularly those of their own students, they will become more moral, more tactful in their teaching. We did encourage interns to gather and analyze information from a variety of sources, most particularly their students, but we might have been more specific about the nature of the data to be obtained. We might have asked them to look at the pedagogical significance of classroom experiences for their students in moral terms and posed for them the "why" questions.

The study does demonstrate that preservice teachers need to be encouraged to think about what works as well as about what does not. They need to examine critically the sources and implications of their beliefs, as well as the outcomes of efforts to implement their ideas. As Hullfish and Smith (1961) argue, they should be "concerned with the process by which beliefs are formed and with the way in which they are held" (p. 110).

Others have made some suggestions as to what might help this process, though all these suggestions are in need of more substantiation.

Smyth (1992), for instance, proposes that teachers ought to be taught to engage in four forms of action that he links to a series of questions: (1) Describe—what do I do? (2) Inform—what does this mean? (3) Confront—how did I come to be like this? and (4) Reconstruct—how might I do things differently? Teitelbaum and Britzman (1991) suggest students need to differentiate interpretations from "objective" observations and delay judgment. This was done in this study, but perhaps not clearly or emphatically enough. Munby and Russell (1992) recommend helping teachers to frame and reframe their educational situations and questions in order to improve reflection; but this strategy, as described, has a general orientation, like the case investigations, and may also need to be directed more specifically toward moral issues to make a difference in that regard.

Liston and Zeichner (1990) see teachers' work as emotionally infused, so "teachers need to maintain a kind of personally engaged but reasonably critical view of schooling" (p. 620). Therefore, "prospective teachers should gain an enhanced understanding of teachers' work, their own experience as teachers, and insight into their relationship with students" (p. 619). Similarly, Beyer (1991) submits that in order to help students develop moral commitments, teacher education programs need to focus more on the affective qualities of moral engagement. In Greene's (1978) words: "We can at least try to surpass what is insufficient and create conditions where persons of all ages can come together in conversation—to choose themselves as outraged and destructive, when they have to, as authentic, passionate, and free" (p. 71). The promise of this perspective, of taking emotions into account in program development and practice, is supported by the presence and operation of the Alert Novice passionate creeds and by the interfering emotional states of interns from both study groups, most especially a subgroup of the Commonsense Thinkers.

Passionate Creeds and Emotional States

The Alert Novices in this study tended to have passionate creeds; they had special missions for their teaching that tended to frame their educational choices and their reflections on those choices. They also tended to serve as an encouragement for engaging in the reflective process; Alert Novices wanted to know how they were doing in relation to those passionate creeds. As with their propensity to ask "why" questions, these students seemed to bring these passions with them.[2] It is possible that the program helped to develop and adapt those passionate creeds, especially given that many program ideas and practices were compatible with these creeds, but such changes were not investigated.

Clues for development can again, however, be culled from these results. Many of the passionate creeds in this study were associated with a particular subject area, for example, the promotion of student voice for the English teacher and the reduction of dogmatism for the social studies teacher. Perhaps passionate creeds might best be fostered in relation to particular subject matters, especially for secondary teachers. This is supportive of the position that teacher educators ought to pay attention to the noneducation coursework of prospective teachers. The nature of the passionate creeds in this study also suggests that the process for learning a particular discipline may be as critical as the content. The creeds have as much to do with how students will go about learning as with what they will learn. Thus subject-matter courses may need to focus more on what Schwab (1964) calls the syntactic knowledge of a discipline. A promising forum for this endeavor within the teacher education program is the "Curriculum and Instruction" or methods course for the subject area, as Grossman's (1990) work seems to indicate. She also suggests that in order for such ideas to be adopted by teacher candidates, they may need to be pervasive and redundant in the program.

More general attitudes toward the educational process might also be candidates for passionate creeds. This study implies, in fact, that one of the purposes of reflective teacher education is to make reflective thinking a passionate creed of all new teachers. Since the processes embedded in many of the creeds seem to be compatible with the processes of reflectivity, attention to the development of reflection in general may go hand in hand with efforts to encourage more specific passionate creeds. Richardson (1990) argues that those of us in teacher education need to "concern ourselves with the content of teachers' reflections, with what teachers will view as problematic" (p. 16).[3] The passionate creeds of the Alert Novices helped to dictate the content of their reflection; thus through the facilitation of particular passionate creeds, teacher educators may find a means for influencing the content of teacher reflection.

This study also demonstrates that the feelings of the individual participant must be considered. This is not only because some emotional traits or states can interfere with the reflective process, but also because emotions are an integral part of reflection and indeed of teaching itself. Dewey (1932) proposes that there is an intimate connection among thinking, emotion, and judgment: "A moral judgment, however intellectual it may be, must at least be colored with feeling if it is to influence behavior" (p. 128). Tomkins, as quoted by Izard (1977), states it well: "Out of the marriage of reason with emotion there issues clarity with passion. Reason without emotion would be impotent, emotion without reason would be blind. The combination of emotion and reason guarantees man's high degree of freedom" (p. 51).

The Commonsense Thinkers need to develop the intrinsic motivation to reflect not only in their teacher education assignments, but beyond. Indeed, all preservice teachers need help in this area, given that the typical conditions they will face in the future are not conducive to reflective thinking. If, as many emotion theorists suggest, emotions not only influence motivation but also "constitute the primary motivational system for human beings" (Izard, 1977, p. 3), an understanding of student teachers' emotional states and traits becomes critical to reflective teacher education. It is not enough simply to present students with knowledge and information and/or with practical experience. Teacher education programs need to concern themselves with the arousal of the appropriate emotions and the reduction of others.

The "why" questions and the passionate creeds together seem to bear some resemblance to what Clandinin (1985) refers to as personal practical knowledge—an emotional and moral knowledge. Her claim is that such knowledge is "intimately connected with the personal and professional narratives of our lives" (p. 385). If such knowledge is indeed closely tied to our personal histories, teacher educators need to attend to the individual if they are to understand and to shape student development in these areas. The results of this study support a need for an individualization of assessment and intervention in teacher education.

Individualization Of Assessment And Intervention

The case investigation score results tend to support the position that initial reflectivity is resistant to change; 78% of the cases written by Alert Novices were rated as reflective in contrast to 22% of those of the Commonsense Thinkers. Though the study cannot answer the root question—"Can reflection actually be taught?"—it does suggest that generic approaches to the educating of reflective teachers are not sufficient. There are several indications, however, that individualized assessments and interventions may yet hold promise for accomplishing the task.

First, my analysis of the thinking processes of the Commonsense Thinkers indicates that entering preservice teachers may be unreflective in different ways and for different reasons. Carole, for instance, seemed to have problems synthesizing various pieces of evidence and information into a coherent conclusion, while Andrea was so lacking in self-confidence that she could not be reflective about any other aspect of her own teaching. These two individuals had entirely disparate needs that called for very different forms of intervention. It is not surprising, then, that simply providing them with opportunities to "practice" reflection was not productive.

But four of the commonsense case investigations were reflective. Three Commonsense Thinkers produced at least one reflective case, representing each of the investigation categories. This demonstrates that the structural variation provided the opportunity for an interaction between the case and the person—a second indication that individualization may be necessary. The teacher case allowed Andrea to focus directly and legitimately on her problems with classroom management and, with the assistance of her observers, her lack of self-confidence. As a result, she was able to recognize the relationship between the two, thus setting the stage for change, or, as in her case, eventual departure from the profession. For Commonsense Thinkers with nonconducive beliefs, values, attitudes, and emotions, reflective tasks may need to include occasions for bringing to the surface and reducing individual interferences. As Van Manen (1991) warns:

> The adult has already become a person with many habits, beliefs, values, feelings, and a history and memory of experiences. If, as adults, we want to try on new modes, to make something different of ourselves, to gain new perspectives, then we may first have to unlearn, unmake ourselves, or integrate new outlooks with our present deeply rooted views. (p. 36)

Old structures may have to be torn down and new ones erected. According to Norman (1982), structuring in this way is the most rare and difficult of the modes of learning, but probably the most important. Unless we make such an effort, reflective teacher education experiences are likely to be miseducative or not educative at all (Holt-Reynolds, 1992).

The three Commonsense Thinkers with inquiry problems were not able to be reflective on any of the assignments, even though all incorporated several features of the reflective process. For these individuals, reflective tasks seem pointless without intensive instruction in the areas of weakness. Houston and Clift (1990) suggest that students ought to be involved in situations that require reflective thinking and then coached through the process, though not in a formulaic way. Diversification is needed not only because individual modes of inquiry vary, but also because "different types of problems necessitate different types of strategies" (p. 218). It may be that the case investigation procedures were too rigid for some students, at least as they were applied in this study.[4] Some might even argue that the whole definition, especially as presented in Figure 1.1, is too prescriptive. However, I believe the accompanying description makes it clear that considerable variation is possible. At any rate the conceptualization does not preclude the context-specific approach to problem solving that Houston and Clift describe, but more attention might still be given to an explicit accommodation of difference, perhaps in the framework, but certainly in program enactment.

The case results for the Alert Novices also support a call for individualization. Since most of the case investigations produced by this group were reflective, the structure of the task did offer the Alert Novices opportunities to practice reflection. Several of them stated in their freewrites and interviews that the assignments had been beneficial, even though they had not always enjoyed the process. Those three who always produced reflective cases had the chance to reflect about a variety of topics in a variety of ways, which, as Richert (1987) observes, may have broadened the content of their reflection and expanded their "repertoire of reflection styles." But there were differences. One of these Alert Novices, Denys, felt that he learned valuable lessons from the student case, whereas Don, another in the group, did not consider the student case to be very productive for him because of his major in adolescent development. These citations not only support the desirability of variety—the "something for everyone" notion—but also corroborate the evidence of an interaction between the person and the task.

My analysis of the four unreflective case investigations produced by the Alert Novices reveals that individualized assessment and support may also be beneficial for these student teachers. The problems Heather and Kim had on the student cases seemed to be caused by emotional interferences similar to those of some of the Commonsense Thinkers. Heather overidentified with her student, making judgments that were based more on her own beliefs and feelings than on her subject's. Kim, in contrast, seemed to maintain such an emotional distance from her student that she was unable to gather the necessary information. Though these obstacles to reflection were not so substantial nor so pervasive as those of Geoff, Andrea, or Rachel, they still caused significant problems in the particular instance.

The other two unreflective case investigations, Laura's student case and Heather's teacher case, appeared to be caused by an overextension of the authors' passionate creeds. Alert Novices with passionate creeds may need help in applying them more discriminately. They also may need inducements to be more analytical about their beliefs—the sources and potential limitations—not because we want them to abandon these commitments (indeed, most seem to be not only noble and sensible, but also incentives to reflection, at least reflection about how well they are doing in relation to their passionate creeds) but because we want them to be more open to reevaluating their creeds in light of new information and new situations. We may have a tendency to overlook this problem in teacher education because the absence of reflective thinking is not so easily detected or so sorely missed when the criteria for judgment employed by the student teacher and the resulting conclusions map well onto current theories and values. Nonetheless, we owe it to these teachers and to their students to continue to push them toward full reflectivity. As Dewey (1932) warned, when the "good" man rests on his oars, his goodness drops away from him.

Hullfish and Smith (1961) also argue in favor of calling into question the individual's fundamental meanings and beliefs; indeed, they consider this inquiry orientation to be the purpose and definition of education. They propose that this can only be accomplished in situations in which the person develops a feeling of incongruency that is not perceived as threatening or overwhelming. Otherwise, defensive thinking and behavior will ensue and prevent the opportunity for growth. Again, this calls for individual examination on the basis of which an appropriately challenging experience can be designed. For several of the Alert Novices, particularly Laura and Denys, the teacher case seemed to operate as such an intervention, but not so for Heather. This case investigation was also most successful, in comparison to the other two, for the Commonsense Thinkers, perhaps because the students had more control over the selection of topics.

I am not the first to make an appeal for individualization in teacher education. Fuller and Bown (1975) made a strong case for the idea several years ago:

> Still, teachers are different from one another. These differences are usually recognized by teacher educators but are rarely provided for in the preparation program. Assignments to education professors, to courses, to laboratory experiences, to supervising teachers, are uniform and random, or intuitive, and are rarely tailored to differing needs in an organized systematic way. (p. 48)

Certainly there are constraints within the structures of teacher education programs that continue to work against such tailoring of assignments. But part of the reason for limited progress may also be insufficient means for determining the nature of the differing needs. This study makes a contribution to the effort through its development of measurement tools and evaluation criteria that can help us to identify reflective strengths and weaknesses. In addition to contributing to our understanding of how teacher education programs ought to be structured and managed, the

findings are suggestive of issues that ought to be considered in the recruitment and admission of preservice teachers and in the assessment of inservice teachers.

RECRUITMENT, ADMISSION, AND ASSESSMENT

This study suggests that the remediation of cognitive and emotional interferences to reflection is not easy. Carole, for instance, never produced a
reflective case. She continued to have difficulty with the examination of
the deeper sources of problems and with the synthesizing of information,
despite the intensive efforts her supervisor claimed to have devoted to this
task and despite her participation in a powerful "English Curriculum and
Instruction" sequence. Of course, it is possible that changes in her reflective thinking did occur but simply did not appear in the case investigations. Although her supervisor's summary evaluation proposes that such
changes did not transpire, his opinions cannot be verified by this study.
Nonetheless, the differences between the outcomes for the Alert Novices
and for the Commonsense Thinkers do suggest that initial reflectivity
tends to remain stable. Like Lloyd, a student teacher studied by Butt and
colleagues (1988), these interns seemed to follow the tendencies framed
by their original patterns of thinking.

If those in charge of teacher education programs agree with me and
with Brenda, "if not a reflective teacher, then never a teacher," these findings may have implications for recruitment and admission. As others
(Banks, 1987; Gore & Zeichner, 1991) have suggested, we might recruit
and select students who are already committed to social justice and who
possess an orientation toward inquiry. The passionate creeds of the Alert
Novices in this study were compatible with program goals and practices
that may have influenced both our selection of them and their selection
of us. Reflective teacher education programs might wish to be very explicit about their goals and commitments in their advertising efforts.

We might use tools such as those employed in this study to assess the
reflective abilities and orientations of novices prior to or in the early
stages of teacher education. This piece of information may be combined
with others to help in decisions about admission and/or advancement. We
may also wish to look for the presence or absence of "passionate creeds"
and at the nature of the questions being asked. Since this was an exploratory study on a very limited and unique population, considerable subsequent research must occur before considering or trying any such changes.
One particular challenge that needs to be addressed is how to obtain ade-

quate information about applicants. Though students could be identified as more or less reflective by an easily administered questionnaire, specific passionate creeds and the nature of the interferences for particular Commonsense Thinkers were only revealed in the comprehensive case studies that incorporated subsequent program experiences as well as entry information. Now that this study has revealed their existence and their importance, however, it should be quite possible to design means for ascertaining more details at the application stage.

The more immediate value of the results of this study in relation to the admission issue is an accentuation of the need to balance our concerns for the results of standardized tests and grade-point averages with attention to the beliefs, values, attitudes, and emotions of our candidates. Not only have we not given these adequate consideration, but our traditional criteria have often served to favor the Commonsense Thinkers (Lanier & Little, 1986; Lortie, 1975). As Fuller and Bown (1975) argue:

> Teachers enter teaching because of a desire for upward mobility, a lack of interest in any other field, and the influence of their elementary and secondary teachers; because education has value to society, because of an interest in a subject matter field, because of opportunities for self-growth, and perhaps because of Stephens' "spontaneous tendencies." Different groups seem to have different motivational patterns but selection procedures do not consider different motivational patterns and may even operate to favor students motivated only by expediency. (p. 36)

This research helps to confirm the need to consider different motivational patterns and helps to reveal what motivational patterns ought to be substituted for "expediency."

Though the subjects in this study were preservice teachers, the results also have implications for the assessment and mentoring of inservice teachers. After all, the focus of this research was on ways to define, measure, and promote reflection, an effort driven by the assumption that reflective thinking is a necessary quality of good teaching. Thus the same theories, task structures, and measurement tools may be useful in helping to determine whether or not more experienced teachers are indeed reflective thinkers. The task is especially important since, according to this study, some preservice teachers do not develop the necessary skills, attitudes, knowledge, or values during the course of their teacher education experience, and since, according to Fuller and Bown (1975), initially reflective novices have a tendency to become more unreflective over time. One of the causes for this unhappy trend is that schools, as they are currently structured, work in opposition to this goal. School restructuring efforts should pay attention to providing the means and the encouragement for reflective thinking; if reflectivity is as important to teaching as I have claimed it is, then concern ought to extend beyond the preservice years. The results of assessments of inservice teacher reflectivity may prove useful in support and remediation, in tenure and promotion decisions, and in potential board certification processes. Again, there is a need for further research on these possibilities before significant changes are made.

IMPLICATIONS FOR RESEARCH

Since this study was exploratory, in a sense the whole of the enterprise is an implication for future research. As such, the need and the possibilities for further investigation have permeated this discussion. A final look at what I consider to be the most significant limitations of this research will help to make next steps more apparent.

First, the social reconstructionist perspective was not prevalent enough in the case investigation assignments or evaluations. Nor was it as pervasive or as explicit as it should have been in program goals or practices. In the future I would modify programmatic structures and strategies to make the development of a moral commitment to justice and humanity more central and more obvious. I might even modify the content segment of the conceptual framework to require that the moral–ethical and social–political be included in every act of reflection.

Second, looks at actual classroom practice were too lacking in this study. Though fieldwork did enter into the case studies in two ways—supervisors gave input on their observations of student teaching, and all case investigations included a practice component, often with outside observers—that was not enough. Clandinin (1985) makes a distinction between verbal expression of images and their expression in classroom practice and argues that "either form of expression may occur without the other" (p. 381). Therefore we cannot judge reflectivity by verbal expressions alone. But, as I have noted before, I agree with Van Manen (1991) that it is possible and worthwhile to look at reflective action apart from thoughtful action. Nonetheless, the true test must be found in interactions between the teacher and the students. A next step for me would be to determine how the "tact of teaching" might be recognized and evaluated.

Third, the study may have been too short in duration. Though data was gathered for the entire length of the credential program (one calendar year), it still might not have allowed sufficient time for registering change. Wildman and colleagues (1990) found that "as teachers became more comfortable and adept at reflection and self-examination, they would turn their attention to a wide variety of problems, taking a much more autonomous posture on how these problems might be solved" (p. 160). Perhaps with more time and practice the Commonsense Thinkers would have begun to exhibit more reflective thinking; of course, the possibility for that may be reduced by the fact that after the program ends, support and encouragement for the process would very likely end as well. Still, efforts to follow student teachers for longer periods of time should be made. Research should be done on the reflectivity of student teachers in reflective teacher education programs that extend over more than one year and on the thinking of graduates of reflective teacher education programs in their first few years of teaching. The results might be suggestive of a need for longer programs or at least longer mentoring periods that would allow reflective processes and propensities to become more natural and more robust.

Fourth, the subjects for this study were few in number and not broadly representative of the student teacher population. Though useful for the generation of theory, those theories now need to be tested in other settings, for example, elementary teacher preparation programs, programs with large numbers of students, and undergraduate programs.

Fifth, this study was limited to an investigation of the nature and stability of reflection in preservice teacher education. Though central to both the content and process of learning to teach, reflection does not constitute everything there is to know or do. The relationship of reflective thinking to other aspects of the teaching profession needs to be better defined and explored.

CLOSING THOUGHTS

Not so very long ago, Maxine Greene (1986) bemoaned the fact that passion was never mentioned with regard to education (p. 78). The tragedy of this absence was that "[a]n emotion, a passion can be a transformation of the world. It can break through the fixities; it can open to the power of possibility. It may even render practice more reflective" (p. 81). The legitimacy of this claim seems to be supported by the case studies of these 12 preservice teachers. Thus I join Greene in calling for more attention to passion in education. Reflective teacher education programs need to incorporate goals and structures that accommodate and address the intricate interaction of emotions, values, attitudes, beliefs, and cognitions in student teacher learning. The results reported in this book should help in this endeavor by providing us with a better understanding of what it is we might mean by reflection in teacher education and how we might go about detecting and facilitating it.

Appendix A

Teacher Case Assignment

Ideally, the process of training reflective teachers involves a gradual transition from more guided reflection to more independent reflection—reflection about various aspects of teaching, including the student, the teacher, instruction, and context. During the summer you focused on the student by doing a case study on an Upward Bound student. This quarter you will focus upon the teacher by doing a guided case study on yourself. In order to do that, we would ask you to do the following things:

1. During one week, a week of your choice, you will keep a journal of your teaching. This can take any form: a freewrite on the day's experiences; a focused analysis of key issues you wish to address; an evaluation of the lessons with ideas for improvement or successes to remember and try again. On one day during that week you need to arrange for your supervisor to make one of his/her usual observations and provide you with written and verbal feedback on one or both lessons. (Remember to do your own journal reflections on those same lessons.) Take notes on the verbal feedback.

2. The following week you will not be keeping the journal. During that week schedule a brief meeting with your supervisor to discuss your journal reflections. You need not share the journal itself, but you might share portions of it, summaries of it, or reactions to it. Talk should focus upon what you are finding; issues that have arisen that you wish to share or have clarified or receive help on; and directions, goals, issues, ideas for the following week. Take notes on the interchange.

3. The next and final week you will again keep a journal of your teaching in the format of your choice. On one day during that week arrange for a fellow student to observe one or both of your classes (which

you need to do for one of your practicum observations anyway; this can count for both). Prior to the observation you should go over with your observer your plans for the lesson. At that time you might even suggest to the observer aspects of your teaching or the classroom that you wish the observer to focus on. The observer should take careful notes on the lesson. At some time, as soon as possible after the lesson, you should talk again about what was observed. Take notes on the discussion. Remember again to do your own journal reflections on the same lesson.

4. At some point after this entire process is over, you will produce a case study on yourself as a developing teacher, based upon the data you have collected—your journal, the observation notes from your colleague and your supervisor, and your discussion notes. The focus of your case study need not be a concern now; you do not need to develop a hypothesis as you did this summer. An idea may come during the process or afterwards as you review your data. Possibilities might include: a consideration of your learning style and its implications for your future development as a teacher; a key incident that occurred during your data collection and your reactions to it; an issue or aspect of your teaching that seemed particularly salient during that time. We will be discussing the write-up further at the November 5 practicum, but if you have any questions or concerns or just wish to chat about "things" as you go, please give a call anytime.

YOUR CASE STUDY WILL BE DUE AT THE FINAL PRACTICUM, WEDNESDAY, DECEMBER 3. AGAIN, PLEASE INCLUDE TWO APPENDICES: APPENDIX 1 — A LIST OF DATA SOURCES AND APPENDIX 2 — A MAXIMUM ONE-PAGE FREEWRITE ON YOUR REACTIONS TO THE EXPERIENCE.

Important Note: At no time during or after this process will you be required to share your journal with anyone. You may be asked if you would like to, but you will not be required to do so. The journal is yours and for your benefit (many of you are already doing something similar anyway, so this will tap right in), and you should feel free to write what and as you wish.

Appendix B

Pre-Study Questionnaire

We have all had extensive experiences in classrooms, as students, and, for some, as tutors or teachers. Research has shown that these experiences have a powerful influence on how we approach the task of learning to teach. Over the course of the year, as a result of both your formal education coursework and your field experiences, many of your conceptions may change. We are interested in studying the nature of those changes. The questions in this test are designed to give us a "base rate" understanding of your conception of what it means to teach and to learn. Please use the paper provided to answer the following questions. Take as much time as you need.

1. Why do you want to teach?
2. What do you want your students to call you (e.g., Miss Wilson, Mr. LaBoskey, Ms. Miller, Harry)? Why?
3. What do you know about this credential program?
4. Why did you decide to enter this program?
5. What do you expect from the program this year?
6. Have you ever taken any education courses? If so, what were they?
7. Have you ever been a teacher or a tutor? If yes, please describe the experience.
8. What kinds of things should teachers know about? That is, if you were to design a test for teachers, what types of information should that exam test for?
9. Define teaching.
10. Define learning.

11. What do you think is the relationship between learning and teaching?
12. Describe what it will be like to be a teacher in a classroom.

In the second portion of this assessment, the student teachers were given oral instructions. They were first shown a portion of a videotaped lesson of a novice English teacher teaching about Animal Farm. *They were then asked to do a brief freewrite reaction to the lesson from the perspective of a student in the class. They saw the same piece of tape again and were asked to do a brief freewrite reaction to the lesson from the perspective of the teacher. Next they were asked to freewrite about who they considered to be the "Best Teacher" they ever had and then who they considered to be the "Worst Teacher."*

Appendix C

Coding Categories for Pre-Study Questionnaire

General Directions

We are looking for the extremes. The most clear-cut responses ought to be rated as +5 or −5. Those that missed the mark or are too difficult to determine ought to be rated as 0. Generally, −5 responses are simplistic and certain; they deal mainly with practical issues and firsthand experience. They see the teacher as the transmitter of knowledge and indicate more concern for themselves and/or the subject matter than the students. In contrast, +5 responses indicate a real struggle with the issues; they show a propensity to consider alternatives and reconsider preconceptions. They indicate greater concern for long-term issues and the needs of students. They seem open to learning both about practical and theoretical ideas. They see the teacher as a facilitator of learning and recognize the complexity of the educational enterprise. [It is important to note that −5 is not necessarily "bad"—the subject may talk about some wonderful things (desirable, idealistic goals and wishes), but in a simplistic, "commonsense" way.]

Specific Directions

Question #2—"What do you want your students to call you (e.g., Miss Wilson, Mr. LaBoskey, Ms. Miller, Harry)? Why?"

[Regardless of choice, the rationale is the indicator.]

−5 Do not see a need for a differentiation of roles; indicate a desire to be friends with the students; portray the adoption of the teacher role as being easy; imply that the title will make the difference. Have not examined the issues—choice made on the basis of tradition.

+5 Indication of a struggle with the issue; they are weighing the various options and are open to possibilities; they understand that the differentiation of roles is an issue, but they are uncertain as to how to do so in a positive, productive fashion. Also, any indication that they accept the new and different role of teacher and that the title may play a part in the development of that role, but this won't be the whole answer (usually a surname choice).

0   Responses that do not answer the question or any response that cannot be rated as −5 or +5

Question #5—"What do you expect from the program this year?"

−5 Focus on the student teaching or field portion of the program and in doing so express interest in recipes rather than frameworks; emphasis on firsthand experience

+5 Mention of theory *and* practice/knowledge *and* experience; indications of growth orientation—desire to learn, to be able to continue to explore and develop over time; interest in frameworks rather than recipes

0   No mention of what or how—talk in generalities, e.g., the program will provide the resources to be an effective teacher; mainly references to the affective—a demanding, fun, rewarding year

Question #8—"What kinds of things should teachers know about? That is, if you were to design a test for teachers, what types of information should that exam test for?"

−5 Fairly simplistic—think the question can be answered with a few discrete, listable skills; almost exclusively relational ("all you have to do is care" implication) and/or practical skill items, e.g., discipline, oral presentation; focus on own experience and imply that teachers are born; teacher as transmitter of subject-matter knowledge; use more as an opportunity to display own knowledge than to probe issue

+5 Indication of awareness of complexity (hard to test); image of teacher as facilitator; any thoughtful discussion of one or more of the following issues: need to adapt subject matter to kids— orientation to student needs; need for "theoretical-type" knowledge; need for flexibility and open-mindedness; need for self-awareness (also if more than one issue identified, they acknowledge the interrelatedness of these issues)

0   Just doesn't clearly go into one of the others, e.g., concentrates on the form of the test; features of the response "cancel each other out," e.g., they have a good list of test-worthy items but they are stated with too much assurance

Question #9—"Define teaching."

[This question is closely related to #10 and #11; these responses should be read at the same time. Though the answers will be rated separately, the ratings may be influenced by one another. Try not to have opposites within these three responses. If two seem to be opposite, consider which seems to be most definite and assign it the + or − score and give the other a 0.]

−5 Teacher as transmitter of knowledge; teaching as doing something to kids

+5 Teacher as facilitator, guide, helper; need for adaptation to learners

0   Generic discussion of the "role of teacher" without reference to the *teaching* of anything or any response that cannot be rated either +5 or −5. Also for this and #10 and #11, if the first reaction is altered by the reading of the two associated responses, give a 0.

Question #10—"Define learning."

[Related to questions #9 and #11. These responses should be read at the same time. Though the answers will be rated separately, the ratings may be influenced by one another.]

−5 Student as receiver of input (learning as just taking in and using); simplistic; reference more to the content than the process and when processes are discussed, they are described as more external than internal, e.g., listening, asking questions; learning as an attitude rather than a process—"being open"

+5 Learning as active process—student in active role with process described as not just acquiring knowledge but adapting, building; active involvement with materials resulting in restructuring of or building upon old knowledge; fairly sophisticated

0   Incomplete answer or one that cannot be rated as either −5 or +5. Also, as in #9, if the first reaction is altered by the reading of the two associated responses, give a 0.

Question #11—"What do you think is the relationship between learning and teaching?"

[This question is related to #9 and #10. However, it can stand well alone and should be rated separately. That is, this question may be read together with #9 and #10 at the time that ratings are assigned to #9 and #10. But the rating for this question should be given at a later time when this question is read again apart from the others. After the rating is decided, check the ratings already given to #9 and #10. If any opposite score is already recorded, all may be reconsidered or a 0 recorded for #11.]

−5 Simplistic—can't have one without the other, especially no teaching without learning, and that's the whole answer; teaching as trans- mission of knowledge; main factor is motivational in whether teaching results in learning; more concern with external behaviors than internal processes

+5 Description of interrelationship of the processes with teaching seen as facilitating learning

0   Talking more about career of teacher than process of teaching; doesn't really answer the question or can't be rated as a −5 or +5

Question #12—"Describe what it will be like to be a teacher in a classroom."

−5 Mainly idealistic, simplistic—lists of tasks; any description that includes other −5 responses, e.g., teacher as transmitter, primary concern with the practical and focus on the self; give the impression of certainty about projections

+5 Picture of continual growth—inquiry orientation; focus on kids more than self; indication of some awareness of +5 concerns, e.g., teacher as a facilitator, education as a complex enterprise

0   Affective description only—a list of emotions or any answer that cannot be rated as −5 or +5

Reaction to a Videotaped Teaching Segment from the Perspective of the Teacher

−5 Practical orientation—centered on teacher behaviors, subject matter (content)–logistics; indications of stereotyping; trouble taking alter- native perspective—focus on self; use question as an opportunity to display own knowledge, especially about the lesson content, *Animal Farm*

+5 Student orientation; concern for bigger, more fundamental questions—the big picture; demonstrate productive reflection about the lesson—asking good questions of themselves about large and small issues

0   Nonserious response or any response that cannot be rated as −5 or +5, e.g., those who have trouble taking the teacher perspective but talk about +5 issues

Appendix D

Post-Study Questionnaire

As the year draws to a close, we would like to take a look at your conceptions of various aspects of education, e.g., teaching, learning, students, schools. We hope this will help you and the program to get a different perspective on what you will take with you from your preservice experience. Take as much time as you need.

1. Why do you want to teach?
2. Define teaching.
3. Define learning.
4. What is the relationship between learning and teaching?
5. If you were ever to leave teaching, what do you think the reason would be?
6. What have you learned about learners this year that has been most useful to you?
7. What kinds of problems have been of most concern to you this year? Give a brief example of one of those problems and your approach to it.
8. This program aims to train reflective teachers. Do you think it does? If so, how? What does it mean to you to be a reflective teacher?

In the second portion of this assessment, the student teachers were given oral instructions. They were first shown a portion of a videotaped lesson of a novice English teacher teaching about Animal Farm. *They were then asked to do a brief freewrite reaction to the lesson from the perspective of a student in the class. They saw the same piece of tape again and were*

148

asked to do a brief freewrite reaction to the lesson from the perspective of the teacher. Next they were asked to freewrite about who they considered to be the "Best Teacher" they ever had and then who they considered to be the "Worst Teacher."

Appendix E

Results of Episode Coding for Alert Novices

		Student			Teacher			Lesson		
		R	U	I	R	U	I	R	U	I
Laura	P	0	1	0	1	0	0	0	1	0
	M	4	3	1	8	0	0	8	3	0
	G	0	1	0	1	0	0	1	0	0
	%	40	50	10	100	0	0	69	31	0
Heather	P	0	1	0	0	0	1	1	0	0
	M	3	10	3	6	6	2	7	4	0
	G	0	3	0	0	1	0	1	1	0
	%	15	70	15	37	44	19	64	36	0
Gwen	P	1	0	0	0	0	1	1	0	0
	M	8	1	2	6	0	0	13	2	2
	G	1	1	0	1	0	0	1	0	0
	%	72	14	14	100	0	0	80	10	10
Don	P	1	0	0	1	0	0	2	0	0
	M	15	2	1	7	3	3	8	0	2
	G	1	0	0	1	0	0	1	1	0
	%	85	10	5	60	20	20	79	7	14
Kim	P	1	0	0	1	0	0	1	0	0
	M	8	4	1	7	2	1	14	1	2
	G	0	2	0	1	0	0	1	0	0
	%	56	38	6	75	17	8	84	5	11
Denys	P	0	1	0	1	0	0	3	0	0
	M	9	2	3	11	1	2	7	1	2
	G	1	0	0	0	0	1	1	2	0
	%	62	19	19	75	6	19	69	19	12

R=Reflective   U=Unreflective   I=Indeterminate
P=Problem setting M=Means–ends analysis G=Generalization

Appendix F

Results of Episode Coding for Commonsense Thinkers

		Student			Teacher			Lesson		
		R	U	I	R	U	I	R	U	I
Rachel	P	0	1	0	0	0	0	0	1	0
	M	6	1	1	2	2	2	4	7	0
	G	1	0	0	1	0	0	0	1	0
	%	70	20	10	42	29	29	31	69	0
Andrea	P	0	0	1	1	0	0	1	0	0
	M	2	4	1	7	0	0	11	8	0
	G	0	0	0	1	0	0	1	0	1
	%	25	50	25	100	0	0	59	36	5
Paula	P	0	1	0	0	1	0	2	0	0
	M	4	6	4	5	5	0	4	11	0
	G	0	1	0	0	1	0	0	1	0
	%	25	50	25	42	58	0	33	67	0
Geoff	P	0	1	0	1	0	0	3	2	0
	M	0	14	1	7	2	2	4	3	0
	G	0	2	0	0	1	0	2	2	0
	%	0	94	6	62	23	15	56	44	0
Beth	P	0	0	0	1	0	0	1	1	0
	M	0	1	0	1	6	2	0	6	1
	G	0	0	0	0	1	0	0	0	0
	%	0	100	0	18	64	18	11	78	11
Carole	P	1	0	0	0	1	0	3	0	0
	M	3	10	2	5	6	3	1	4	0
	G	0	1	0	0	1	0	1	2	0
	%	23	65	12	31	50	19	45	55	0

R=Reflective   U=Unreflective   I=Indeterminate
P=Problem setting   M=Means–ends analysis   G=Generalization

Notes

1. I designed three of the four case investigations used in this study. The fourth was already in use in one of the required courses and was designed by the professors of that course.

2. Supervisors during this year were all doctoral students at the university. They were trained by me in eight two-hour weekly sessions that summer in both general processes of supervision and in skills associated with the facilitation of the case investigation assignments.

3. In a limited number of cases involving special circumstances, I was the respondent. For instance, one student's supervisor was also the teacher for the Upward Bound class her subject had attended, and the paper included some criticism of the supervisor's teaching; so the student asked me to be the reader.

4. This fieldwork can consist of two student teaching periods, two internship periods, or one of each. For the purposes of ease of communication, the terms *student teacher* and *intern* are used interchangeably to refer to all participants in this study.

5. Even though the student population was expected to be quite reflective on entrance, the pretest indicates that in general the novices were more unreflective than reflective.

6. Because extreme scores were selected from a single test administration, there is the danger of measurement error and regression to the mean. This potential threat to the reliability of the study was addressed in two ways. First, the supervisor evaluations of reflectivity served to corroborate or, in one case, call into question the placement of the participants into the Alert Novice or Commonsense Thinker categories. Second, this weakness was acknowledged throughout and given overt attention in each of

the individual case summaries: A systematic attempt to locate confirming and disconfirming evidence for each placement was undertaken.

7. To protect the identity of the informants, all the names used in this document are pseudonyms.

8. There was one other with a score of +15. Since only two of the three with that score were needed to define the six Alert Novices in the study, numbers were drawn from a hat to insure that the decision was unbiased.

9. Freewriting is a technique wherein individuals write for a certain period of time without stopping to ponder a thought or to consider spelling, punctuation, or grammar. The person puts down whatever comes to mind (Macrorie, 1984).

10. One informant, Laura, did not submit hers until the following summer, after the program was over. The time difference was not a significant factor in this study because the questionnaires were not used to evaluate development over time.

11. To check the reliability of the coding of episodes, I asked another researcher, unfamiliar with the process, to code a subset of the cases. I gave her a brief overview of the scoring procedures and presented her with copies of the coding criteria for each of the cases and the general directions for episode coding. The inter-rater reliability for the first run-through was 62%. We met again to review in detail the coding procedures in relation to the six cases she had scored and to clear up any confusions or differences in interpretation. The inter-rater reliability after the second run-through was 82%.

CHAPTER 3

1. In one sense the "improvement over time" construct is not appropriate to this analysis at all because the three case structures are so different from one another. However, since a fundamental aim of the program is to facilitate reflection, there is an implicit assumption that participating student teachers will be more reflective when they leave the program than when they entered. Thus they should do better on later tasks designed to encourage and reveal reflection than on early ones. Furthermore, since little attention has been given to the importance of the specific structure of those tasks, as Richert (1987) documents, there seems to be an additional implicit assumption that this development in reflectivity might be detectable wherever it occurs. These assumptions, fairly widespread in reflective teacher education, are in part what this study is designed to investigate.

2. The number of episodes recorded within each category do not match across tables because in some displays the mixed scores were separated out and in others they were not.

CHAPTER 4

1. It is unclear whether Beth was referring to the two students interviewed, the whole class, or students in general.

2. Andrea began this case study with the (anonymous) quote: "Two prisoners looked outside their window; one saw bars and the other saw stars."

CHAPTER 5

1. Laura did not respond to the post-study questionnaire until the summer after the program had ended. The others in the study were done after about nine months of the twelve-month program had been completed.

2. Multiple additional examples are cited throughout this volume.

3. There are several instances in the data that seem to indicate that Kim may have overprotected herself from "knowing" students who might have been particularly problematic in the student case. The associated freewrite is the most directly relevant example of this: "I learned that I have a tendency to deny myself from doing things that are enjoyable and not valuing them as highly as I should. By this, I mean that I really enjoyed the time I spent with Coyote and the other Upward Bound (UB) students, but I didn't spend nearly enough time with them. Rather, I felt pressured to do other 'serious' schoolwork. I felt a sense of loss when UB ended because I had been somewhat removed." Another example, which appears in her teacher case investigation freewrite, was cited earlier. She talked about not wanting to reflect too much, particularly about "the tragic lives led by our students," because then one may wonder "whether we're perhaps in the wrong profession." After praising her in abundance, Kim's supervisor said this of her in his summary evaluation: "The bionic teacher? Perhaps so. Especially because, like Dorothy's Tin Man, the one thing she lacked was a heart . . . at least a vulnerable heart."

4. The difference may be representative of the difference of emotional states and emotional traits in Izard's (1977) terms. He defines the former as limited in duration and the latter as "a tendency of the individual to experience a particular emotion with frequency in his day-to-day life" (p. 5).

CHAPTER 6

1. Brenda (a pseudonym) was one of the original 50 participants, but not one of the final 12 case study subjects.

2. The compatibility between initial passionate creeds and program goals and practices may say something about why students decided to enter this particular program. This possibility will be discussed in the section on recruitment and admission.

3. Richardson also argues that research on the reflective teacher education process ought not be too positivistic. Though the case studies in this research are not, the case investigation scoring might seem so. This might need to be modified to incorporate more flexibility, as will be noted in the section on individualization.

4. Many subsequent renditions of case investigation assignments have incorporated greater opportunity for individual modification and adaptation.

References

Adler, S. (1991). Forming a critical pedagogy in the social studies methods class: The use of imaginative literature. In B. R. Tabachnick & K. M. Zeichner (Eds.), *Issues and practices in inquiry-oriented teacher education* (pp. 77–90). London: Falmer.

Anzul, M., & Ely, M. (1988). Halls of mirrors: The introduction of the reflective mode. *Language Arts, 65*(7), 675–687.

Applegate, J., & Shaklee, B. (1992). Stimulating reflection while learning to teach: The ATTEP at Kent State University. In L. Valli (Ed.), *Reflective teacher education: Cases and critiques* (pp. 65–81). Albany: State University of New York Press.

Baird, J. R. (1992). Collaborative reflection, systematic enquiry, better teaching. In T. Russell & H. Munby (Eds.), *Teachers and teaching: From classroom to reflection* (pp. 33–48). London: Falmer.

Banks, J. A. (1987). The social studies, ethnic diversity, and social change. *The Elementary School Journal, 87*(5), 531–541.

Barnes, D. (1992). The significance of teachers' frames for teaching. In T. Russell & H. Munby (Eds.), *Teachers and teaching: From classroom to reflection* (pp. 9–32). London: Falmer.

Beyer, L. E. (1991). Teacher education, reflective inquiry and moral action. In B. R. Tabachnick & K. M. Zeichner (Eds.), *Issues and practices in inquiry-oriented teacher education* (pp. 113–129). London: Falmer.

Bissex, G. L. (1988). On learning and not learning from teaching. *Language Arts, 65*(8), 771–775.

Bolin, F. S. (1987, April). *Students' conceptions of teaching.* Paper presented at the annual meeting of the American Educational Research Association, Washington, DC.

Borko, H., Livingston, C., McCaleb, J., & Mauro, L. (1987, April). *Student teachers' planning and post-lesson reflections: Patterns and implications for teacher preparation.* Revised version of a paper presented at the annual meeting of the American Educational Research Association, Washington, DC.

Boud, D., Keogh, R., & Walker, D. (1985). Promoting reflection in learning. In D. Boud, R. Keogh, & D. Walker (Eds.), *Reflection: Turning experience into learning* (pp. 18–40). New York: Nichols.

Britzman, D. P. (1986). Cultural myths in the making of a teacher: Biography and social structure in teacher education. *Harvard Educational Review, 56*(4), 442–455.

Britzman, D. P. (1989). Who has the floor? Curriculum, teaching, and the English student teacher's struggle for voice. *Curriculum Inquiry, 19*(2), 143–162.

Bromley, D. B. (1986). *The case-study method in psychology and related disciplines.* Chichester, England: Wiley.

Brown, J. S., Collins, A., & Duguid, P. (1989). Situated cognition and the culture of learning. *Educational Researcher, 18*(1), 32–42.

Buchmann, M., & Schwille, J. (1983). Education: The overcoming of experience. *American Journal of Education, 92*(1), 30–51.

Bullough, R. V., & Gitlin, A. D. (1991). Educative communities and the development of the reflective practitioner. In B. R. Tabachnick & K. M. Zeichner (Eds.), *Issues and practices in inquiry-oriented teacher education* (pp. 35–55). London: Falmer.

Butt, R., Raymond, D., & Yamagishi, L. (1988). Autobiographic praxis: Studying the formation of teachers' knowledge. *Journal of Curriculum Theorizing, 7*(4), 87–155.

Calderhead, J. (1988). Learning from introductory school experience. *Journal of Education for Teaching, 14*(1), 75–83.

Calderhead, J. (1989). Reflective teaching and teacher education. *Teaching and Teacher Education, 5*(1), 43–51.

Candy, P., Harri-Augstein, S., & Thomas, L. (1985). Reflection and the self-organized learner: A model of learning conversations. In D. Boud, R. Keogh, & D. Walker (Eds.), *Reflection: Turning experience into learning* (pp. 100–116). New York: Nichols.

Ciriello, M. J., Valli, L.,& Taylor, N. E. (1992). Problem solving is not enough: Reflective teacher education at the Catholic University of America. In L. Valli (Ed.), *Reflective teacher education: Cases and critiques* (pp. 99–115). Albany: State University of New York Press.

Clandinin, D. J. (1985). Personal practical knowledge: A study of teachers' classroom images. *Curriculum Inquiry, 15*(4), 361–385.

Clandinin, D. J. (1989). Developing rhythm in teaching: The narrative study of a beginning teacher's personal practical knowledge of classrooms. *Curriculum Inquiry, 19*(2), 121–141.

Clandinin, D. J., & Connelly, F. M. (1991). Narrative and story in practice and research. In D. A. Schön (Ed.), *The reflective turn: Case studies in and on educational practice* (pp. 258–281). New York: Teachers College Press.

Clift, R. T., Houston, R. W., & McCarthy, J. (1992). Getting it RITE: A case of negotiated curriculum in teacher preparation at the University of Houston. In L. Valli (Ed.), *Reflective teacher education: Cases and critiques* (pp. 116–135). Albany: State University of New York Press.

Clift, R. T., Houston, W. R., & Pugach, M. C. (Eds.). (1990). *Encouraging re-*

flective practice in education: An analysis of issues and programs. New York: Teachers College Press.

Cruickshank, D. R. (1987). Reflective teaching: The preparation of students of teaching. Reston, Virginia: Association of Teacher Educators.

Cruickshank, D. R., Kennedy, J. J., Williams, E. J., Holton, J., & Fay, D. E. (1981). Evaluation of reflective teaching outcomes. Journal of Educational Research, 75(1), 26–32.

Dewey, J. (1904). The relation of theory to practice in education. In C. A. McMurry (Ed.), The relation of theory to practice in the education of teachers (Third yearbook of the National Society for the Scientific Study of Education, Part I). Chicago: University of Chicago Press.

Dewey, J. (1910). How we think. Boston: D. C. Heath and Co.

Dewey, J. (1932). Theory of the moral life. New York: Holt, Rinehart and Winston.

Donmoyer, R. (1985). The rescue from relativism: Two failed attempts and an alternative strategy. Educational Researcher, 14(10), 13–20.

Elbaz, F. (1983). Teacher thinking: A study of practical knowledge. London: Croom Helm.

Erickson, G. L., & MacKinnon, A. M. (1991). Seeing classrooms in new ways: On becoming a science teacher. In D. A. Schön (Ed.), The reflective turn: Case studies in and on educational practice (pp. 15–36). New York: Teachers College Press.

Feiman-Nemser, S., & Buchmann, M. (1985). Pitfalls of experience in teacher preparation. Teachers College Record, 87(1), 53–65.

Feiman-Nemser, S., & Buchmann, M. (1987). The first year of teacher preparation: Transition to pedagogical thinking? (Research Series No. 156). Michigan State University: The Institute for Research on Teaching.

Fenstermacher, G. D. (1986). Philosophy of research on teaching: Three aspects. In M. C. Wittrock (Ed.), Handbook of research on teaching, Third Edition (pp. 37–49). New York: Macmillan.

Frijda, N. H. (1987). Comment on Oatley and Johnson-Laird's "Towards a cognitive theory of emotions." Cognition and Emotion, 1(1), 51–58.

Fuller, F., & Bown, O. (1975). Becoming a teacher. In K. Ryan (Ed.), Teacher education (The seventy-fourth NSSE yearbook). Chicago: University of Chicago Press.

Gardner, H. (1983). Frames of mind: The theory of multiple intelligences. New York: Basic Books.

Goodman, J. (1984). Reflection and teacher education: A case study and theoretical analysis. Interchange, 15(3), 9–26.

Goodman, J. (1991). Using a methods course to promote reflection and inquiry among preservice teachers. In B. R. Tabachnick & K. M. Zeichner (Eds.), Issues and practices in inquiry-oriented teacher education (pp. 56–76). London: Falmer.

Gore, J. M. (1987). Reflecting on reflective teaching. Journal of Teacher Education, 38(2), 33–39.

Gore, J. M. (1991). Practicing what we preach: Action research and the supervision of student teachers. In B. R. Tabachnick & K. M. Zeichner (Eds.), *Issues and practices in inquiry-oriented teacher education* (pp. 253–272). London: Falmer.

Gore, J. M., & Zeichner, K. M. (1991). Action research and reflective teaching in preservice teacher education: A case study from the United States. *Teaching and Teacher Education, 7*(2), 119–136.

Greene, M. (1978). *Landscapes of learning.* New York: Teachers College Press.

Greene, M. (1986). Reflection and passion in teaching. *Journal of Curriculum and Supervision, 2*(1), 68–81.

Grimmett, P. P. (1988). The nature of reflection and Schön's conception in perspective. In P. P. Grimmett & G. L. Erickson (Eds.), *Reflection in teacher education* (pp. 5–15). New York: Teachers College Press.

Grimmett, P. P., MacKinnon, A. M., Erickson, G. L., & Riecken, T. J. (1990). Reflective practice in teacher education. In R. T. Clift, W. R. Houston, & M. C. Pugach (Eds.), *Encouraging reflective practice in education: An analysis of issues and programs* (pp. 20–38). New York: Teachers College Press.

Grossman, P. L. (1990). *The making of a teacher: Teacher knowledge and teacher education.* New York: Teachers College Press.

Heron, J. (1985). The role of reflection in a co-operative inquiry. In D. Boud, R. Keogh, & D. Walker (Eds.), *Reflection: Turning experience into learning.* New York: Nichols.

Hollingsworth, S. (1989). Prior beliefs and cognitive change in learning to teach. *American Educational Research Journal, 26*(2), 160–189.

Holt-Reynolds, D. (1992). Personal history-based beliefs as relevant prior knowledge in course work. *American Educational Research Journal, 29*(2), 325–347.

Houston, W. R., & Clift, R. T. (1990). The potential for research contributions to reflective practice. In R. T. Clift, W. R. Houston, & M. C. Pugach (Eds.), *Encouraging reflective practice in education: An analysis of issues and programs* (pp. 208–222). New York: Teachers College Press.

Hullfish, H. G., & Smith, P. G. (1961). *Reflective thinking: The method of education.* New York: Dodd, Mead.

Izard, C. E. (1977). *Human emotions.* New York: Plenum.

Kagan, D. M. (1992). Professional growth among preservice and beginning teachers. *Review of Educational Research, 62*(2), 129–170.

Kemmis, S. (1985). Action research and the politics of reflection. In D. Boud, R. Keogh, & D. Walker (Eds.), *Reflection: Turning experience into learning* (pp. 139–163). New York: Nichols.

Kitchener, K. S. (1983). Educational goals and reflective thinking. *The Educational Forum, 48*(1), 75–96.

Kitchener, K. S. (1986). The reflective judgment model: Characteristics, evidence, and measurement. In R. A. Mines & K. S. Kitchener (Eds.), *Adult cognitive development: Methods and models* (pp. 76–91). New York: Praeger.

Korthagen, F. (1985). Reflective teaching and preservice teacher education in the Netherlands. *Journal of Teacher Education, 36*(5), 11–15.

Korthagen, F., & Verkuyl, H. (1987, April). *Supply and demand: Towards differ-*

entiation in teacher education based on differences in learning orientations. Paper presented at the annual meeting of the American Educational Research Association, Washington, DC.

LaBoskey, V. K. (1992). Case investigations: Preservice teacher research as an aid to reflection. In J. H. Shulman (Ed.), *Case methods in teacher education* (pp. 175–193). New York: Teachers College Press.

Lanier, J. E., & Little, J. W. (1986). Research on teacher education. In M. C. Wittrock (Ed.), *Handbook of research on teaching* (3rd ed.) (pp. 527–569). New York: Macmillan.

Leeper, R. W. (1969). A motivational theory of emotion to replace "emotion as disorganized response." In K. H. Pribram (Ed.), *Brain and behavior 4: Adaption* (pp. 349–372). Middlesex, England: Penguin.

Leventhal, H., & Scherer, K. (1987). The relationship of emotion to cognition: A functional approach to a semantic controversy. *Cognition and Emotion, 1*(1), 3–28.

Liston, D. P., & Zeichner, K. M. (1990). Teacher education and the social context of schooling: Issues for curriculum development. *American Educational Research Journal, 27*(4), 610–636.

Lortie, D. C. (1975). *Schoolteacher: A sociological study.* Chicago: University of Chicago Press.

Maas, J. (1991). Writing and reflection in teacher education. In B. R. Tabachnick & K. M. Zeichner (Eds.), *Issues and practices in inquiry-oriented teacher education* (pp. 211–225). London: Falmer.

Macrorie, K. (1984). *Writing to read.* Upper Montclair, NJ: Boynton/Cook.

Main, A. (1985). Reflection and the development of learning skills. In D. Boud, R. Keogh, & D. Walker (Eds.), *Reflection: Turning experience into learning* (pp. 91–99). New York: Nichols.

McCaleb, J., Borko, H., & Arends, R. (1992). Reflection, research, and repertoire in the Masters Certification Program at the University of Maryland. In L. Valli (Ed.), *Reflective teacher education: Cases and critiques* (pp. 40–64). Albany: State University of New York Press.

Miles, M. B., & Huberman, A. M. (1984). *Qualitative data analysis: A sourcebook of new methods.* Beverly Hills: Sage.

Morine-Dershimer, G. (1987, April). *Research to revision to research: A revolving-door approach to innovation in teacher education.* Paper presented at the annual meeting of the American Educational Research Association, Washington, DC.

Munby, H., & Russell, T. (1992). Frames of reflection: An introduction. In T. Russell & H. Munby (Eds.), *Teachers and teaching: From classroom to reflection* (pp. 1–8). London: Falmer.

Noffke, S. E., & Brennan, M. (1991). Student teachers use action research: Issues and examples. In B. R. Tabachnick & K. M. Zeichner (Eds.), *Issues and practices in inquiry-oriented teacher education* (pp. 186–201). London: Falmer.

Noffke, S. E., & Zeichner, K. M. (1987, April). *Action research and teacher thinking: The first phase of the action research on action research project at the University of Wisconsin–Madison.* Paper presented at the annual meeting of the American Educational Research Association, Washington, DC.

Nolan, J. F., & Huber, T. (1989). Nurturing the reflective practitioner through instructional supervision: A review of the literature. *Journal of Curriculum and Supervision, 4*(2), 126–145.

Noordhoff, K., & Kleinfeld, J. (1990). Shaping the rhetoric of reflection for multicultural settings. In R. T. Clift, W. R. Houston, & M. C. Pugach (Eds.), *Encouraging reflective practice in education: An analysis of issues and programs* (pp. 163–185). New York: Teachers College Press.

Norman, D. A. (1982). *Learning and memory.* New York: Freeman.

Oatley, K., & Johnson-Laird, P. N. (1987). Towards a cognitive theory of emotions. *Cognition and Emotion, 1*(1), 29–50.

Oja, S. N., Diller, A., Corcoran, E., & Andrew, M. D. (1992). Communities of inquiry, communities of support: The five year teacher education program at the University of New Hampshire. In L. Valli (Ed.), *Reflective teacher education: Cases and critiques* (pp. 3–23). Albany: State University of New York Press.

Palincsar, A. S., & Brown, A. L. (1984). Reciprocal teaching of comprehension-fostering and monitoring activities. *Cognition and Instruction, 1,* 117–175.

Parsons, J. B. (1983). Towards understanding the roots of reflective inquiry. *The Social Studies, 74*(2), 67–70.

Peters, R. S. (1969). Emotion, passivity and the place of Freud's theory in psychology. In K. H. Pribram (Ed.), *Brain and behavior 4: Adaption* (pp. 373–394). Middlesex, England: Penguin.

Pugach, M. C., & Johnson, L. J. (1990). Developing reflective practice through structured dialogue. In R. T. Clift, W. R. Houston, & M. C. Pugach (Eds.), *Encouraging reflective practice in education: An analysis of issues and programs* (pp. 186–207). New York: Teachers College Press.

Putnam, J., & Grant, S. G. (1992). Reflective practice in the Multiple Perspectives program at Michigan State University. In L. Valli (Ed.), *Reflective teacher education: Cases and critiques* (pp. 82–98). Albany: State University of New York Press.

Reyes, D. J. (1987). Cognitive development of teacher candidates: An analysis. *Journal of Teacher Education, 38*(2), 18–21.

Richardson, V. (1990). The evolution of reflective teaching and teacher education. In R. T. Clift, W. R. Houston, & M. C. Pugach (Eds.), *Encouraging reflective practice in education: An analysis of issues and programs* (pp. 3–19). New York: Teachers College Press.

Richert, A. E. (1987). *Reflex to reflection: Facilitating reflection in novice teachers.* Unpublished doctoral dissertation, Stanford University, Stanford, CA.

Richert, A. E. (1992). The content of student teachers' reflections within different structures for facilitating the reflective process. In T. Russell & H. Munby (Eds.), *Teachers and teaching: From classroom to reflection* (pp. 171–191). London: Falmer.

Ross, D. D. (1987). Action research for preservice teachers: A description of why and how. *Peabody Journal of Education, 64,* 131–150.

Ross, D. D. (1990). Programmatic structures for the preparation of reflective teachers. In R. T. Clift, W. R. Houston, & M. C. Pugach (Eds.), *Encouraging reflective practice in education: An analysis of issues and programs* (pp. 97–118). New York: Teachers College Press.

Russell, T., & Munby, H. (1991). Reframing: The role of experience in developing teachers' professional knowledge. In D. A. Schön (Ed.), *The reflective turn: Case studies in and on educational practice* (pp. 164–187). New York: Teachers College Press.

Russell, T., & Munby, H. (Eds.). (1992). *Teachers and teaching: From classroom to reflection.* London: Falmer.

Russell, T., Munby, H., Spafford, C., & Johnston, P. (1988). Learning the professional knowledge of teaching: Metaphors, puzzles, and the theory–practice relationship. In P. P. Grimmett & G. L. Erickson (Eds.), *Reflection in teacher education* (pp. 67–90). New York: Teachers College Press.

Schlechty, P. C., & Vance, V. S. (1983). Recruitment, selection, and retention: The shape of the teaching force. *Elementary School Journal, 83,* 469–487.

Schoenfeld, A. H. (1985). *Mathematical problem solving.* Orlando, FL: Academic Press.

Schön, D. A. (1983). *The reflective practitioner: How professionals think in action.* New York: Basic Books.

Schön, D. A. (1987). *Educating the reflective practitioner.* San Francisco: Jossey-Bass.

Schön, D. A. (1988). Coaching reflective teaching. In P. P. Grimmett & G. L. Erickson (Eds.), *Reflection in teacher education* (pp. 19–29). New York: Teachers College Press.

Schön, D. A. (Ed.). (1991). *The reflective turn: Case studies in and on educational practice.* New York: Teachers College Press.

Schwab, J. J. (1964). The structure of the disciplines: Meanings and significances. In G. W. Ford & L. Pugno (Eds.), *The structure of knowledge and the curriculum* (pp. 6–30). Chicago: Rand McNally.

Schwab, J. J. (1978). The practical: Translation into curriculum. In I. Westbury & N. J. Wilkof (Eds.), *Science, curriculum, and liberal education* (pp. 229–272). Chicago: University of Chicago Press.

Shulman, L. S. (1986a). Paradigms and research programs in the study of teaching: A contemporary perspective. In M. C. Wittrock (Ed.), *Handbook of research on teaching* (3rd ed.), (pp. 3–36). New York: Macmillan.

Shulman, L. S. (1986b). Those who understand: Knowledge growth in teaching. *Educational Researcher, 15*(2), 4–14.

Shulman, L. S. (1988). The dangers of dichotomous thinking in education. In P. P. Grimmett & G. L. Erickson (Eds.), *Reflection in teacher education* (pp. 19–30). New York: Teachers College Press.

Shulman, L. S., & Carey, N. B. (1984). Psychology and the limitations of individual rationality: Implications for the study of reasoning and civility. *Review of Educational Research, 54*(4), 501–524.

Sinnott, E. (1966). *The bridge of life.* New York: Simon & Schuster.

Smyth, J. (1992). Teachers' work and the politics of reflection. *American Educational Research Journal, 29*(2), 267–300.

Sparks-Langer, G. M., & Colton, A. B. (1991). Synthesis of research on teachers' reflective thinking. *Educational Leadership, 48*(6), 37–44.

Tabachnick, B. R., & Zeichner, K. (1984). The impact of the student teaching on the development of teacher perspectives. *Journal of Teacher Education, 35,* 28–42.

Tabachnick, B. R., & Zeichner, K. M. (Eds.). (1991). *Issues and practices in inquiry-oriented teacher education.* London: Falmer.

Teitelbaum, K., & Britzman, D. P. (1991). Reading and doing ethnography: Teacher education and reflective practice. In B. R. Tabachnick & K. M. Zeichner (Eds.), *Issues and practices in inquiry-oriented teacher education* (pp. 166–185). London: Falmer.

Tom, A. (1985). Inquiry into inquiry-oriented teacher education. *Journal of Teacher Education, 36*(5), 35–44.

Valli, L. (1990). Moral approaches to reflective practice. In R. T. Clift, W. R. Houston, & M. C. Pugach (Eds.), *Encouraging reflective practice in education: An analysis of issues and programs* (pp. 39–56). New York: Teachers College Press.

Valli, L. (Ed.). (1992). *Reflective teacher education: Cases and critiques.* Albany: State University of New York Press.

Vance, V. S., & Schlechty, P. C. (1982). The distribution of academic ability in the teaching force: Policy implications. *Phi Delta Kappan, 64*(1), 2–27.

Van Manen, M. (1977). Linking ways of knowing with ways of being practical. *Curriculum Inquiry, 6,* 205–228.

Van Manen, M. (1978). Objective inquiry into structures of subjectivity. *Journal for Curriculum Theorizing, 1*(1), 44–64.

Van Manen, M. (1991). *The tact of teaching: The meaning of pedagogical thoughtfulness.* Albany: State University of New York Press.

Walker, D. (1985). Writing and reflection. In D. Boud, R. Keogh, & D. Walker (Eds.), *Reflection: Turning experience into learning* (pp. 52–68). New York: Nichols.

Weade, G. (1987, April). *Negotiating a culture: The preservice teacher's socialization into reflective teaching practice.* Paper presented at the annual meeting of the American Educational Research Association, Washington, DC.

Webster's Ninth New Collegiate Dictionary. (1984). Springfield, MA: Merriam-Webster.

Wehlage, G. G. (1981). Can teachers be more reflective about their work? A commentary on some research about teachers. In B. R. Tabachnick, T. S. Popkewitz, & B. B. Szekely (Eds.), *Studying teaching and learning* (pp. 101–113). New York: Praeger.

Wildman, T. M., & Niles, J. A. (1987). Reflective teachers: Tensions between abstractions and realities. *Journal of Teacher Education, 38*(4), 25–31.

Wildman, T. M., Niles, J. A., Magliaro, S. G., & McLaughlin, R. A. (1990). Promoting reflective practice among beginning and experienced teachers. In R. T. Clift, W. R. Houston, & M. C. Pugach (Eds.), *Encouraging reflective practice in education: An analysis of issues and programs* (pp. 139–162). New York: Teachers College Press.

Yin, R. K. (1984). *Case study research: Design and methods*. Beverly Hills: Sage.

Zeichner, K. M. (1981–82). Reflective teaching and field-based experience in teacher education. *Interchange, 12*(4), 1–22.

Zeichner, K. M. (1983). Alternative paradigms of teacher education. *Journal of Teacher Education, 34*(3), 3–9.

Zeichner, K. M., & Liston, D. (1987). Teaching student teachers to reflect. *Harvard Educational Review, 57*(1), 23–48.

Zeichner, K. M., Liston, D. P., Mahlios, M., & Gomez, M. (1987, April). *The structure and goals of a student teaching program and the character and quality of supervisory discourse*. Paper presented at the annual meeting of the American Educational Research Association, Washington, DC.

Zeichner, K. M., & Tabachnick, B. R. (1991). Reflections on reflective teaching. In B. R. Tabachnick & K. M. Zeichner (Eds.), *Issues and practices in inquiry-oriented teacher education* (pp. 1–21). London: Falmer.

Index